# CORPORATIONS 101

## A GUIDE FOR BEGINNERS

# DAVID EGAN

*CORPORATIONS 101*
*A Guide for Beginners*

Copyright © 2019 by David Egan

eBook 978-0-578-49618-4
Print 978-0-692-06515-0

Interior Format by The Killion Group, Inc.

# TABLE OF CONTENTS:

# I: INTRODUCTION

*"Go to school, get a job."*

W E'VE ALL HEARD IT. IT'S the American way. My journey with this phrase started at a very young age. With both parents college educated and working for a major oil company in Houston, Texas, it was beaten into my subconscious mind that only one path existed in life—finish school and work for a major corporation. This would ensure my acceptance into society and alleviate any risk associated with achieving something outside the standard protocol of its firmly established norms.

So, off I went. I made my way through elementary school, then junior high, high school, and eventually college. To top it off, I finished graduate school for an MBA—exactly what the "American way" stated I should be doing. Eager to put my education to use, I landed a job with a Fortune 100 company. But then something strange occurred. Once inside a corporation, I realized the technical foundation my degree provided was only part of the equation. My success relied on yet another knowledge set, one hidden far below the tangible surface of academia's overpriced text books and never-ending PowerPoint lectures. It was a psychological corporate code or sorts, one whose obedience to, or lack thereof, seemingly dictated the trajectory of every individual's career within the organization. Blindsided by its presence, I realized my education had failed me.

But why is something so incredibly important to one's success never mentioned during four years of higher

education? ~~Because colleges teach skills that make~~ cor-
~~porations more successful—not ones that make *you*~~ *more*
~~*successful within them*~~. This means thousands of graduates
walk away each year with a degree that taught them absolutely nothing about what it takes to succeed within one.
My goal is to fill that hole.

The idea for this book came about in a fairly unique
way. At the time of this writing, I am still employed by
the same Fortune 100 company I began my career with
over twelve years ago. My initial dreams were to someday achieve an executive level position, a path not all that
unreasonable given my ambitions as an early professional.
But life apparently had other plans. A year or two into
my career, I noticed my unique ability to both observe
and dissect the psychological structure my company was
built upon. Fascinated by its presence, I began untangling
its intricate details and watched as my coworkers battled
haplessly against its invisible forces. A few were naturals
and never missed a beat, almost as if they were born to
play the corporate game. The rest were not so fortunate, crashing at every turn, never to fully understand
nor appreciate the breadth of enemy which they were up
against.

It was then when I felt a push from within to document
my observations. And for the next seven years, I did just
that. Without any idea what I would use them for, I took
a few minutes each evening to notate my observations
throughout the workday. After amassing over sixty pages
of scribbled notes, I still had no clear vision for their use.
My initial thoughts were to use them as fodder for giving
career advice to younger employees. It wasn't until my
early thirties after going through a rough patch that their
true purpose was revealed—to share them with the entire
world. And many years and thousands of hours later, here
I present what I hope to be one of the most helpful guides
ever written for early professionals entering a major cor-

poration for the first time.

That said, let's get started. But as you read, please keep in mind that at the end of the day, I'm just a normal guy with a finance degree trying to get my crazy ideas down on paper. Some may strike you as the nuttiest things you have ever heard. But if you learn just one thing from this book I will consider it a success.

# II: YOUR FIRST DAY - GET YOUR HEAD STRAIGHT

LET'S GET SOMETHING CLEAR UP front. Once inside a major corporation, that 4.0 GPA you worked so hard to achieve is now utterly and unequivocally worthless. Yes, worthless. From here out, all that matters is what can you do *today*. But make no mistake. Landing your first job is a big achievement and should be celebrated accordingly. So, enjoy it while you can. Why? Because life as you knew it is over. Your priorities will now shift from making sure the pizza guy gave you enough parmesan cheese to surviving the most intense psychological battlefield you will ever encounter.

To be honest, your first day inside a corporation is terrifying. You are at the bottom of the totem pole. You cannot go any lower. And worse, the entire corporation will be observing your every move. They will watch when you arrive, when you leave, and how long you take during bathroom breaks. Ok, in all seriousness, it will be nothing like what I just described. Relax! Corporations today are more laid back and flexible than ever before. Executives have realized that in order to survive, they must adjust to the newer generation of employees, even if that means allowing for ping pong during work hours.

What does that mean for you? It means you have more power than you think. You are the future of these companies and to remain in business they must continually promote the next generation of leaders into management positions to backfill those who retire. That said, heed these words. The decisions you make within your first six months will undoubtedly be the most important ones of your entire career. Why? Because you will unknowingly be categorized in one of two buckets. Not three, not four, not five. Two buckets. The "potential leader" bucket, and, the "no chance in hell" bucket. Your placement within these buckets will determine the initial trajectory of your career. And once set, its course is near impossible to change. It's similar to dating. You must avoid the friend zone at all cost, especially if you have the potential to be much more.

How do you avoid the wrong bucket? By making your expectations clear from day one. Don't go out for coffee when you really want champagne. By settling for coffee, the expectation going forward is that you have no interest in champagne. You will be placed in the "friend zone" and the corporation will move on to someone else, all because you failed to clearly communicate what your goals were. This mistake must be avoided at all cost, especially if seeking higher paying management jobs. You must be explicitly clear when communicating your ambitions. The corporation will determine these ambitions using a very simple process. *They'll ask you.* And, it will happen shortly after you step inside the door.

"So, Mr. Jimmy, what are your career goals and aspirations?"

Sounds innocent enough, right? Wrong—this is a loaded question. Do not ever, and I mean ever, say "I don't know". You may not have an honest clue but you must have a solid answer even if it's bullshit. Large corporations have enormous numbers of candidates to sift through. This question is used as an initial filter to categorize who their potential leaders are. Respond right, go to the good bucket. Respond wrong, get ready for admin work. But be careful. Forcefully declaring your plans to become CEO could make you look arrogant rather than ambitious. Instead, impress them with conviction.

"I'll go as far as my talents will take me and am fully prepared to do whatever it takes to get there". Simple as that. No more, no less. Memorize this and have it ready at all times.

Now that we have that out of the way, let's move on. There are four stone cold facts true about every corporation on this planet which you must familiarize yourself with. I had to learn these the hard way, as did most others. Having this knowledge in your back pocket from day one will be a major advantage.

<u>Fact #1</u>

*Only one person inside your corporation*
*gives a damn about you.*
*That person is YOU.*

When brand-new to a company, this can be hard to grasp—especially if wined and dined as part of an extravagant recruitment process. After such an experience, you may believe you are entering a land of fertile fields where you'll be immediately praised as the company's next great leader. That is, until you realize the individuals recruiting you were professionals who make their living bringing people like you into the company. Once locked in, you become worthless to them. They were only pretending to care about you, the first of many who will do so.

The truth is corporations can be cold, nasty, bloody places. Will there be people that help you, guide you, coach you? Absolutely. You may even make some great friends along the way. But you must understand that business is not always pretty. Every corporation goes through

8 DAVID EGAN

rough patches. It's during these times when those friends become rivals as their focus turns to survival. It's only then when you realize your work environment isn't as chummy as it once seemed. *Never be fooled.* People are there to put food on their table, to pay their bills, to buy their wives or husbands fancy gifts. ~~They are not going to put your friendship ahead of those things.~~

~~People work in corporations for their own personal gain, not yours.~~ Never believe you can depend on anyone else besides yourself to succeed. That includes your bosses. Will they make you believe they care about your success? Of course. The more valued you feel, the more you will produce. The more you produce, the better they look as a manager. This means bigger bonuses and juicier steaks for them. The truth is you're nothing more than a disposable resource which they can and will discard at a moment's notice should you fail to help further their career. Don't ever believe that you're anything more. After all, who's going to look after you when they transfer to another division, never to be seen again? ~~You are.~~ And believe me, it happens *all* the time. Later in the book I will provide more detail on this topic. For now, just remember to always watch your six—nobody else will do it for you.

<u>Fact #2</u>

~~*You are an asset.*~~

After completing my MBA in May of 2006, I landed a job with one of the largest defense contractors in the world. My first role was incredible. I managed all the finances for a department which conducted initial test flights on brand new fighter jets as soon as they rolled off the production line. I was twenty-three at the time and surrounded by fifteen of the best fighter pilots in the country on a daily basis. My desk was located within a building that stood roughly ten feet from the flight tower. Every time a jet would take-off, the walls would rattle so hard it felt as if they were collapsing. During my breaks, I would climb to the top of the tower and watch every imaginable type of military aircraft take-off and land. I could not have asked for a more exciting job.

There was one day in particular I will never forget, a day when my company was flying a newly designed fighter for the first time. In the defense contracting world, there is no bigger achievement. There are years and sometimes decades of design and development that go into these aircraft prior to them actually flying. This one was no exception—eleven years had passed since the initial plans were constructed. That said, we were extremely excited as it would be an enormous achievement given the significant technological breakthroughs this aircraft was capable of. And me? I was right in the middle of the action.

Given my vicinity to the flight tower, I had seen many test flights before and was quite familiar with the routine. Pilots would arrive thirty minutes prior to their anticipated flight time for final equipment and weather checks. Knowing this, I decided to head over. But when I arrived, I quickly realized this was no ordinary test flight. I was witnessing history and was standing right next to the pilot who was about to make it. He was about to fly for the first time what would likely be the last manned fighter jet in the history of the world. *Wow.*

The point is this. No matter how cool this jet was, it wasn't going anywhere until he climbed inside and pushed the throttle. It was impossible. He was just as important to the company's success as it was. This is because he, along with every piece of machinery and tool used to build the aircraft, was an *asset*.

In corporations, people aren't viewed as people. Rather, as assets. And, corporations want a return on those assets just as they would anything else they invest their money into. Similar to a piece of equipment, the more you produce, the better the corporation will maintain you through raises and promotions. But should you not produce, the opposite will occur. Like a faulty piece of equipment, you will be treated like scrap and relegated to the corner where you will sit and collect dust. When it comes time for a "clean out", you're as good as gone. To survive in a corporation, you must *always* be producing. The pilot standing next to me that day was about to produce at the highest levels possible.

Fact #3

*Corporations cannot be successful
without capable leaders guiding them.*

What do corporations and shrimp boats have in common? They are both dependent on something besides themselves to function in their intended capacity. What does that mean? Think about it. What good is a shrimp boat that has no captain? It's worthless. It will do nothing but sit at the dock. This isn't what shrimp boats are made for. They are made to be on the water, catching monster-loads of fresh shrimp. But without a captain providing guidance, it will fail in its mission one hundred percent of the time.

How does this relate to corporations? A corporation without leadership is like a shrimp boat without a captain. Without it, it will never satisfy the requirements of its original design—to produce returns for its shareholders. It makes no difference whether the corporation is making fuzzy remote control covers or creating a cure for cancer. You see examples of this all the time. Take cell phone providers for example. These are commodity companies who offer the exact same product, yet one is often demolishing the other. How can this be? It all comes down to the captain in charge. Company A's captain places their team right on top of the shrimp, day in and day out. Their boat is no different than the other company's—everything from the engine, to the paint, and even the crew. Company A is just better at exploiting their boat's strengths while guarding against its weaknesses. They know their rig and they know their crew. But more importantly, they know precisely how to combine them to create a lean, mean shrimp-catching machine.

But what about company B? The crew is soaked and exhausted after their captain spun them in circles all day *trying* to find the honey hole. By the time they got to fishing, they had zero motivation to do so as their energy had long been drained. Do you see where I'm going? The two boats had the exact same specs, the exact same passengers and the exact same mission—to catch shrimp. Captain A was just better prepared for the mission.

This is why corporations must remain fully staffed with competent "captains". Doing so keeps the business right on top of the honey hole at all times. But make no mistake. This caliber of employee is few and far between, oftentimes leaving corporations no choice but to gamble on someone having what it takes to succeed in one of these positions. But this is incredibly risky. If they gamble wrong, the boat will go in circles all day looking for the honey hole instead of driving straight to it, wasting valuable time and resources. Terrible financial performance and angry shareholders won't be far behind.

The bottom line is that without a proper captain creating a seamless harmony between the boat (i.e. the business), and its crew (i.e. the employees), the boat will do nothing but burn valuable resources, time, and employee morale. And if you burn employee morale, you burn motivation. And once motivation goes, so goes their desire to catch shrimp. No shrimp, no profits, no business. Make sense?

## Fact #4

### *The Highest Offer Isn't Always the Best Offer*

Money is without a doubt the greatest evil you will ever encounter. On one hand, it has the power to let you live comfortably and enjoy what's important—family, friends, and a few hobbies. But severe consequences are always nearby should it control you. Wasteful spending, ruined relationships, unintended debt, and gambling addictions, just to name a few. It's a trap millions fall into every year and one that can be incredibly hard to avoid. However, it can be prevented by prioritizing what you value. Keep family and friends at the top and be safe from its pitfalls forever. Prioritize materialistic items and prepare for a rough road ahead.

Regardless of how you value money, there's one constant which remains certain. You won't make much of it right after college. So, swallow this pill now because it will make evaluating job offers a much easier task. I'm now going to describe two scenarios. Picture each and decide which you would rather live your life by.

### Scenario One:

*You're stuck on a cold and windy island with your worst enemy. The island is infested with large, aggressive African army ants. However, you have a servant to meet your every need. The island is stocked with an unlimited supply of fresh lobster, chocolate, and champagne, along with an exquisitely furnished bungalow perched over the water.*

## Scenario Two:

*You're stuck on a warm and tranquil island with your ten best friends. You live off hand caught fish and fresh fruit. You spend your evenings inside a meager but sturdy cabin made of sticks and palm fronds. You have no servant, but the island is free of African army ants and you spend your days rolling around in the beautiful sand.*

Which scenario would you choose? Many would take option one because you are given an unlimited supply of expensive lobsters and chocolate to eat. But consider, the rest of your life is a long time to spend on an island, especially one you're miserable on. I'm not saying this offer doesn't look appealing at first, which is where most get themselves into trouble. But after one month, the only thing on your mind will be figuring a way to get off this island as fast as you possibly can. There will be no amount of juicy lobsters on Earth that can to convince you to stay. The ants are too much to overcome.

Do not ever take an offer just because it is a few bucks higher than the next offer. Do your homework. If the lower offer is with a reputable company who provides better career growth opportunities, odds are it will be a better choice when looking at the bigger picture. Choosing otherwise may send you into a professional hell where there's no such thing as raises or career advancement. Can you switch companies after realizing your mistake? Yes, but valuable time will be wasted re-establishing yourself which could have been avoided had you just picked wisely to begin with. It's the equivalent of giving your opponents a two-lap head start.

Don't get me wrong. You can never be absolutely certain you're choosing the correct offer. But you can lower the risk of a miscalculation by doing your research and listening to mentors who understand your chosen profession. They have been around the block and can smell a rat far earlier than you. For instance, if I didn't listen to my dad regarding an offer I received from a small bank just prior to the great recession in the late 2000's, I would have accepted and been laid off not one year later when the bank closed its doors. The offer was higher than what my current employer was willing to pay; however, he was able to foresee the economic turbulence ahead and guided me towards not only a better company which provided greater long-term value, but to an industry that also happened to be recession-proof.

Another reason not to be caught up with starting salaries is they are only that—*starting*. What happens down the road is far more important.

Let's do some quick math. What is seven percent of $50,000? Answer: $3,500. What about seven percent of $100,000? Answer: $7,000. The same percentage was applied in both examples yet scenario two generated a one-hundred percent increase. It's the power of compounding returns, and it applies just as much to salaries as it does to investing in the stock market.

Here's how it works. In many corporations, every year your performance will be assessed. Based on the results, you will earn what's called a "merit" raise. These are derived from your prior year's performance and issued in the form of a percentage increase to your base salary. In theory, the better you perform, the higher your percent will be and vice versa. But as a new employee, this can be very frustrating. Your salary is still relatively low and the resultant dollar increase can be discouraging. At first, that is.

Enter the power of compounding returns. As the years pass, your base salary will slowly become bigger, leading to larger salary increases even while the applied percentage remains constant. Without this knowledge, you may falsely believe your seven percent raise when making $50,000 isn't that much better than your peer who receives three percent. After all, it's only a $2,000 difference. But if you fast forward ten years, the story changes drastically.

Let's say you consistently outperform your peer year after year and continue receiving seven percent raises while they remain steady at three percent. Guess what the salary difference is then? Just take a look below.

| | 7% Raise | 3% Raise | % Difference |
|---|---|---|---|
| Year 1 | $50,000 | $50,000 | 0% |
| Year 2 | $53,500 | $51,500 | 4% |
| Year 3 | $57,245 | $53,045 | 7% |
| Year 4 | $61,252 | $54,636 | 11% |
| Year 5 | $65,540 | $56,275 | 14% |
| Year 6 | $70,128 | $57,964 | 17% |
| Year 7 | $75,037 | $59,703 | 20% |
| Year 8 | $80,289 | $61,494 | 23% |
| Year 9 | $85,909 | $63,339 | 26% |
| Year 10 | $91,923 | $65,239 | 29% |
| Year 11 | $98,358 | $67,196 | 32% |
| Year 12 | $105,243 | $69,212 | 34% |
| Year 13 | $112,610 | $71,288 | 37% |
| Year 14 | $120,492 | $73,427 | 39% |
| Year 15 | $128,927 | $75,629 | 41% |

Look at year ten. At this point, your salary will be a whopping twenty-nine percent more than your peer. You will be making $92k while they are at $65k. Now look at year fifteen—the power of compounding is in high gear. You are absolutely obliterating them, making an astounding $129k while they are at $76k, an astonishing $53k difference (which is more than your original salary to begin with). And given your stellar performance, odds are you were promoted several times throughout those fifteen years which means this variance could be even larger.

To summarize, your beginning days inside a major corporation are some of the most important of your entire career. Treat them like an artist would a blank canvas. Some will splatter paint everywhere. Others will create masterpieces that sell for millions. It's completely up to you how your painting will turn out. Nobody is going to paint it for you. And guess what? You don't have an eraser. Once you make a stroke there's no going back. There's only one time in your career when you're given a blank canvas to work from. That time is now. Tread carefully.

# III: THE CORPORATE "SKI LIFT"

CORPORATIONS CANNOT MOVE FORWARD WITHOUT employees. Never in history has there been a business run entirely by robots that didn't need some level of human involvement. This poses a major problem for them. Why? Because humans have shelf lives. We're all going to die. There are no ifs, ands, or buts about it. It's just a fact of life. Corporations on the other hand, as we know from prior history, can continue on for many decades or longer. But to do so, they must continually cycle employees throughout its ranks to fill vacancies created by those who transfer into other positions or leave the company entirely. If not, they will be forced to close their doors as there will be nobody left to carry them forward.

To put this in perspective, let's go back to one of the greatest inventions of all time. On October 1st, 1908, Henry Ford introduced the Model T, the first affordable automobile made available to the American public. It sold a mind-boggling fifteen million units within twenty years of its release. Fast forward to April 7th,1947. Ford sadly passes away from a cerebral hemorrhage at the age of eighty-three. By that time, most of his employees had also died or were at the end of their lives, forcing the company to reduce production to fifty units a year. Ford would eventually shut its doors, never to make another car again.

As we're all aware, that's not what happened. (Relax historians!) Ford is still around today and is doing tremendously well. But how can this be? They had in place what's referred to as succession plans. These are a company's blueprints that determine how they go about dealing with employees who not only leave the company entirely but also those promoted within it, both which create a vacancy within the organization. Should a corporation streamline these plans, they can essentially eliminate the impact of an employee leaving their position by ensuring someone will always be available to immediately replace them. Think of them as insurance policies that corporations take out against their employees. The employee is the item insured and the premium is the cost the corporation pays to guarantee a backup will be available should that employee ever vacate their post.

Now, it's not cheap for corporations to implement these plans. Oftentimes they are left with fully trained and underutilized employees sitting in what I refer to as "corporate holding patterns" waiting for others above them to move on before they can take their slot. But that is a pill most corporations are willing to swallow as the impact of not having a trained replacement far exceeds any cost required to have them there to begin with. If a key position opens up and nobody is available to fill it, a company could be looking at substantial levels of operational disruption along with productivity gaps, both which add significant amounts of cost to the bottom line. But they must be careful not to keep employees waiting for too long as they may become impatient, causing them to leave for another opportunity. Or worse, they could remain at the company but suffer low morale given the lack of growth opportunities, leading to a drop-off in their productivity. On a grand scale with many employees involved, this, too, can become expensive for a corporation. It would be like an auto-repair shop hiring a fleet of fully trained auto mechanics but only tasking them with oil changes. Eventually they will lose interest and disengage themselves, driving cost higher as more mechanics will be needed to fill the gaps created by those who are no longer producing at the required levels.

This is precisely why the best companies manage their succession plans as they would a just-in-time inventory system. For those not familiar, just-in-time inventory is the practice of minimizing the holding time of an asset, whether it be raw material, finished products, or an employee, so it becomes ready and available only when required by the company and not a day earlier. This lowers the company's holding costs of such assets, freeing up capital to spend elsewhere on other revenue generating projects. In terms of a company's employees, this means their development must be timed so that growth opportunities become available only when an individual is ready for them, ensuring they remain not only in a state of engagement right up to the point of promotion, but growth as well. This is an area we will cover in much greater detail later in the book.

Now that we understand the importance succession plans and their role in safeguarding a corporation's longevity, lets discuss the mechanics behind how they actually operate. It's very similar to a ski lift. The purpose of a ski lift is to pick skiers up at one level of the mountain and drop them off at another somewhere further up. What makes them unique is these pick-ups and drop-offs occur at the *exact same time*. With regards to a corporation, this translates to hiring, promoting, and retiring employees all at once. But most importantly, it's a non-stop process that never ends.

The one major difference between an actual ski lift and a corporate ski lift is speed at which they run at. With an actual ski lift, there's only one speed. But in a corporation, running at only one speed isn't an option as it could potentially create a situation where the company is either hiring too many or too few workers, leading to a disconnect in the level of resources required to satisfy the demands for the company's products. To avoid this, corporations must continually alter the speed at which they run their lift. This ensures their "mountain" will remain staffed at levels perfectly aligned with current business demands. This is where corporations operate at peak efficiency. However, effectively managing these speeds is much easier said than done. Many companies fail miserably at it, creating productivity gaps within the organization that drives costs higher and profits lower for reasons I will soon explain.

But how does a company know what their "magic speed" is? Is there a secret machine that spits out reports showing executives how much to open or close the faucet? No. But it doesn't take a rocket scientist to figure it out. It's similar to portion control with food. Someone who isn't an active person doesn't need to eat as much as someone who hits the gym every day. But if they continue eating large portions anyways, they'll gain weight, causing them to become slow and sluggish. Without proper intervention their bodies will eventually fail. Businesses are no different in this regard. They, too, can fail as a result from eating too much. It's just caused by overstaffing, not overstuffing.

To help explain, let's say you graduated college and had the ambition to start an amazing business soon after graduation. During your senior year you realized there was a huge need for a fuzzy boat seat. No one had ever made one before and you were certain that your product was going to revolutionize the boat seat market. All your friends thought you lost your marbles, and rightfully so. Fast forward twelve months. You tuned out the naysayers and spent an entire year making the fuzzy seats in your parents' garage. And guess what, you couldn't make them fast enough! Word about your product quickly spread and orders began flowing in. To keep up with the demand, you decided to go big. You moved into a warehouse, set up a production line, hired twenty-five employees and bought a dozen water coolers to keep your staff freshly hydrated. Over the next several years, you continually increased your staff to meet demand as business continued to boom. You quickly hit one hundred employees, then two hundred, three hundred, and eventually, you had over one thousand people on your staff. *You were essentially filling your mountain with skiers.*

Before you knew it, you were living the dream life. You had a wonderful business, family, home, cars, boats, jet skis, etc. You had it all. You won yard of the month for six consecutive months and even considered running for city mayor. But you would soon be faced with your biggest challenge yet—*competition*. Up to this point, it was nonexistent. You patented your product in the early days preventing any potential competitors from entering the market. But all patents expire. When this day came, the market was immediately flooded with competitors which sent sales into a rapid and steady decline. You, my friend, were in big trouble. Your staff started showing up later, going home earlier, and sitting around all day instead of filling orders. Why? Because you didn't have enough business to keep them busy anymore. In the corporate world, this is referred to as being *fat*.

You had one of three options to get the ship back on course. You could continue running your ski lift at the same pace it ran for the last ten years, bringing new employees into the company consistent with the rate your business *was* growing at. But doing so would have only made your company even more sluggish, further eating into an already reduced level of profitability. This obviously wasn't an acceptable solution.

The next option was to slow the ski lift down, reducing the inflow of new employees. Similar to losing "weight", this technique requires slowing the input to more closely align with business demands until such time that equilibrium regains control. Think of it as the balance point on a see saw. A company will run at peak efficiency when one side no higher than the other. This is achieved by reducing the number of employees entering the company to a level which is lower than the number exiting via retirements and transfers. In the corporate world, this is called "natural attrition".

While slowing the lift and tapering the inflow of new employees will stabilize a company over time, there are some instances where companies don't have that convenience and must implement immediate and decisive solutions. The most common being one you never want to experience as an employee within a major corporation. *Layoffs.* While not frequent, they are necessary when the demand for a company's product suffers a drastic and unexpected drop off. Several circumstances can lead to such an event. The loss of a major contract, or, if a commodities company, a significant reduction in the price of the underlying commodity (oil for example). These occurrences can bankrupt a business and must be resolved without delay.

Being overweight isn't the only problem a company can have. They can also be too lean. In other words, not having enough employees to fulfill the company's demand for its products. This can be just as detrimental as customers will inevitably become frustrated causing them to leave for a competitor, never to be seen again. Companies will make every adjustment necessary to avoid this outcome. Increasing the "nutrients" flowing into the organization by speeding up their ski lift is a one way to accomplish this. It's like giving water to someone dying of dehydration. As increased fluids are provided, their bodies will slowly return to equilibrium. Starving businesses are no different. They are a living organism where input and output must be harmonized to achieve maximize performance. Businesses across the globe pay tens of millions every year for consultants to help them do this very thing. Disguised by catchy buzzwords nobody can understand, these consultants all target the same underlying principles. Optimize the input, optimize the output, or optimize the relationship between the two.

The moral is that every business must run their lift at speeds which keep their staffing levels synchronized with the current output demand. But that isn't the only variable which must be managed when it comes to the corporate ski lift. Companies must also manage how high (or low) each employee is brought up the mountain, placing them at the level best suited for their individual skills and experience. Poor execution can inflict the same level of damage as running the lift at incorrect speeds. To clarify, take a look at the diagram below.

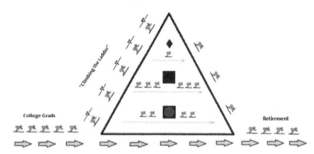

Let's begin with the skiers on the far left who are heading towards the mountain. These are your recent college graduates entering the company for the first time. They represent the never-ending flow of human capital which every corporation must have in order to stay in business indefinitely. And the skiers on the far right? Those are the newly minted retirees who are happily moving on to the next stage of their lives. And last but not least, the skiers actually on the mountain. They represent the company's current employees who fall into one of three groups.

*Group One:*
The skiers at the bottom by the green circle.

These are your non-ambitious types who aren't overly concerned with dedicating their entire life to the corporation and are content staying at the lower levels. This by no means implies they are any less smart than those who make it further up. They may actually be the smartest employees in the corporation by recognizing the key to life isn't found at the top of the mountain, but at the bottom. It's here where low stress is achieved and time with family is maximized. But make no mistake. While the work done at these levels is important, it usually requires far less talent or experience and comes with the lowest levels of pay within the organization.

*Group Two:*
The skiers in the middle by the blue square.

These employees worked their butts off and became skilled enough to ski from the blue slopes. Keeping the rubber on the road, they are known as the "grinders" within the corporation. They embrace challenges and make up the largest segment of the employee population. The work accomplished here is done by experienced professionals who aren't easily replaceable and command higher salaries than those on the green slopes below them.

*Group Three:*
The skiers at the top by the black diamond.

Comprising the smallest group on the mountain, these employees consist mainly of executive level employees. Possessing a relentless work ethic, they leave nothing on the table and spend their entire adult lives dedicating everything they have to their craft. To successfully ski down these slopes, an immense knowledge base is required which is attained by spending many years within the lower ranks of the company.

In a real corporation, there will certainly be more "levels" than the three I described above. But whether it's three or three hundred, each serves a distinctly different purpose regarding the output of the business. Therefore, never assume the work accomplished on the bottom isn't critically important just because the employees doing it don't have the drive or intellect to make it further up. It's actually the exact opposite. If their work doesn't get done, then none of the work above gets done.

Let me explain further. Below is Maslow's hierarchy of needs.

Maslow's hierarchy states there are five levels of basic human needs, all which are interdependent upon each other and must be satisfied in a strict sequence. And, it applies just as much to corporations as it does life. If the work at the bottom doesn't get done by the grinders, then the prettier, more sophisticated work above will never be completed as its foundation is rooted by the work being done below.

But if you're anything like me when first starting your career, you couldn't care less about what makes up the hierarchical structure within corporations. The only thing that matters is climbing to the top in the quickest way possible. But I must give an honest warning. While higher levels do come with more pay, they also come with extreme sacrifices—long hours, high stress, and time away from your family, just to name a few. So, before you become starry-eyed by the thought of a massively larger paycheck, you must be fully aware the corporation will get every dollar of it out of you. It's safe to say many executives were enticed by the money only to regret taking the job because of what it cost them personally. Unfortunately for them, this realization comes far too late when they are stuck with no way out, forcing them to ride it out or retire early.

So, you have been warned. But as I mentioned before, if you were anything like me right out of school, this warning will go in one ear and out the other. Yup, completely and utterly meaningless. But that's fine, you have bills to pay. It's entirely understandable. However, you must realize that money follows experience and not the other way around. Why is that? Because higher paying jobs within corporations come with responsibilities that require experience across the lower levels in order to be successful within them. No matter how smart or qualified you may be, building this experience takes time.

In "ski lift" terms, this translates to the corporation booting you off the lift before you reach a slope which they deem too difficult for you. But what if they let you up to the black diamond slope anyways? What would happen then? If it were a real ski slope, you would crash headfirst into a tree due to your inexperience. The only damage inflicted would be upon yourself. But in corporations, black diamond slopes are much, much different in this regard. These top positions carry immense levels of political power and financial responsibility. If you crash and burn in one of them, it will certainly impact the bottom line which could affect hundreds, if not thousands, of other people and possibly destroy your career. Some lucky executive will then have to explain to investors why this person was allowed on that slope to begin with when they didn't have the necessary experience to ski down it. That isn't a conversation any executive wants to have.

Where does this leave you as a new employee? If you want to advance off the green slopes, don't focus on the money. Focus on the *experience*. This is by far the most counterintuitive thing you will ever have to learn regarding how corporations operate, especially if you have the brains to handle larger positions but lack the necessary experience required to be promoted into them. Incredible patience is required to persevere through these times.

Just like your paycheck, your experience levels will start slow. But as you gain more, it will compound and feed off itself. It's at this time when the corporation will allow you access to the more difficult slopes higher up the mountain. But remember, corporations care about one thing. *Themselves.* Not your spouse, not your newborn, not your college debt, and certainly not your feelings. What they do care about is how much value you can provide to the bottom line. If they feel you can provide more of it in a higher-ranking job than what you're currently in, they'll move you up. *Simple as that.*

Here's a quick review. First, for corporations to continue on forever, they must continually cycle employees throughout their ranks. The speed at which this is done must be closely managed to remain consistent with current output demand. Next, the work accomplished on one level of a corporation is dependent upon the work being done at another. And finally, for you to be allowed up to the higher, more difficult slopes on the mountain, you must first gain the required experience throughout the lower levels. When these experiences are consolidated, you can then provide greater value in a more seasoned position. It's at this moment when the company will be *forced* to promote you as taking any other course of action would be leaving untapped value on the table.

What does all this mean for you as a new employee? *It means you have more power than you think.* Corporations are in a continual battle with time, twenty-four hours a day, three hundred sixty-five days a year. Time is by far the most powerful force on this earth. No single man, organization, or military has ever been strong enough to defeat it. To survive, corporations must go with time, not fight it. This is the essence behind the corporate ski lift and is what allows businesses to stay alive for indefinite periods without being restricted by their employees "expiration dates". Time is also what gives you, as a young employee, all the power. Without you, *they cannot survive.* But that doesn't guarantee your success. You must still position yourself so when the corporation hands over the keys to the next generation that you're the one who gets them. And how do you make sure you're that person? The rest of the book is going to focus on just that.

# IV: RESPECT — SEE THE INVISIBLE

I ALWAYS ENJOY BUSINESS ARTICLES EXPLAINING the proper way to ask for a raise. For the most part, they all say the same thing.

*If your boss isn't recognizing your contributions, inform them of your efforts and request that you be compensated accordingly.*

Now, my interest in these articles isn't because I think they are informative. Rather, because I'm constantly amazed by the damage they inflict upon their readers. How so? By falsely inflating self-worth and instilling belief that they are under-compensated, leading them to engage in drastic and destructive behaviors. Storming into the boss's office demanding immediate compensation increases doesn't end well for the employee. Nevertheless, these tactics do work on rare occasion; however, this strategy is deeply flawed regarding how you should go about asking for a promotion inside of a major corporation. Why? Because it puts the power of promotion in your boss's hands, *not your hands.*

When seeking a raise or promotion in a major corporation, it should be approached in a way that minimizes your boss's role to nothing more than a figurehead signing the paperwork. This is accomplished by indirectly overpowering their authority to where they have no other choice *but* to promote you as taking any other course of action would not only cause the corporation to suffer, but their career as well. This is what it means to keep the power of promotion in your hands, not theirs. For the rest of the chapter I will describe how to do just that.

To help explain, I'm going to bring in one of my all-time favorite pastimes. Watching prison shows. *Lockup, Lockdown, On Death Row, The Big House,* you name it. What first began as late-night entertainment spiraled into outright addiction as I became fascinated by the psychological hierarchy within prisons and the various forms of brutality which shaped them. It wasn't until working in a major corporation for several years that I connected the dots and realized that when it came to large organizations of people, whether it be in prisons or elsewhere, that an invisible ranking system always existed. It's just established through different means. But once determined, the result is always the same—an invisible pecking order within the ranks, otherwise known as the dominance hierarchy.

Wikipedia states that a dominance hierarchy *"arises when members of a social group interact, often aggressively, to create a ranking system. Members are likely to compete for access to limited resources and mating opportunities. Rather than fight each time they meet, relative relationships are formed between members of the same sex. These repetitive interactions lead to the creation of a social order that is subject to change each time a dominant member is challenged by a subordinate one."*

This is the absolute truth of why certain individuals are promoted within major corporations and others aren't. The key is to gain rank within the dominance hierarchy. In prisons, this is accomplished by fighting, stabbing, and even killing each other. These behaviors obviously won't fly in a corporation. Employees must therefore resort to more traditional tactics such as outthinking, outsmarting, and outwitting each other. Their level of success employing these tactics will either increase or decrease their ranking within the hierarchy, otherwise known as their *level of respect* within the corporation. (More on how to achieve this respect in the next chapter. The focus for now is on the invisible power structure behind promotional decisions.)

I will now restate Wiki's definition. This time I'm going to make a few adjustments to show you how it relates to corporations.

*"A corporate dominance hierarchy arises when employees within a corporate environment interact, often aggressively, to create a ranking system. In corporate peer groups, members are likely to compete for limited promotion and growth opportunities. But rather than compete each time they meet, relative relationships are formed between each member of the group. This leads to the creation of a professional order that is subject to change each time a dominant employee is challenged by a subordinate one."*

Each year, thousands of eligible employees are passed over for promotions, never to understand why. Overflowing with technical ability, they fail to realize that meeting the tangible requirements alone isn't enough. With only so many promotions to go around, there will be many others who also meet those same requirements. So, who goes up and who doesn't? Does the boss randomly decide? The boss's boss? The boss's boss's boss? No, no, and no. Bosses have nothing to do with making this determination. It's made solely on the basis of the organization's dominance hierarchy, and more specifically, where each employee ranks within it.

The reason corporations rely on the dominance hierarchy is because it highlights those who carry the most valuable skill in all of business—the ability to influence. Others not only listen to these individuals, but *respond* to them as well. In prison gangs, these are shot callers— the ones who ensure their fellow gang members remain focused on the important targets. Without them, the gang would have no guidance, pursuing every target in sight, unintended ones included.

This is precisely why you will never go straight into management right out of college without first establishing your ranking within the dominance hierarchy. It poses too much risk for the corporation to do so. Will some companies gamble and send you up anyways? Sure. But this isn't the norm and usually happens only when no other options are available. A miscalculation could lead to unguided employees wandering aimlessly around obstructing themselves and others. Corporations avoid this by patiently allowing the dominance hierarchy to evolve. Whoever rises to the top is then "plucked" and reassigned into a higher-level position where they can exert their influence in an official capacity.

One mistake many corporations make is ignoring the dominance hierarchy all together and basing their decisions purely on an employee's productivity levels as an individual contributor. They automatically assume this same level of productivity will permeate itself onto an entire team of people once made responsible for them. This couldn't be further from the truth. To be a successful leader, you must first have the respect of the people you are leading. If not, it's like running an engine without oil. It just doesn't work. Employees will disobey and output will tank. But when managers are respected, it's a much different story. Employees will jump higher, run faster, and reach further. The best corporations understand this and capitalize by promoting individuals into leadership positions who their employees *already* respect. Doing so all but eliminates any risk of noncompliance from employees when a new manager is promoted over them. This is where the dominance hierarchy excels. It gives corporations the ability to "test the goods" before making significant investments in the form of management level salaries and bonuses.

As simple as this may seem, making promotion decisions based off an organization's dominance hierarchy is no easy task. Counterintuitive at its core, successful implementation relies not on action, but rather inaction. Wait for the pieces to slide into place and react accordingly. That's all corporations have to do. The problem arises when they become impatient and force things by placing employees with zero influence into positions of power and/or leave high-potential employees stuck within the lower ranks. Both scenarios hurt the business as those individuals become either under- or over-stretched in terms of the value they are capable of providing.

Earning rank within the dominance hierarchy is only half the equation when earning a promotion within a major corporation. And unfortunately, the other half is something you have absolutely zero control over—the corporation's demand for someone of your abilities. You may have heard the phrase "success happens when preparation meets timing". Both must be aligned for success to occur. In corporate speak, this means you won't automatically become a manager just because you are fully prepared to be one.

To explain further, think back to your Economics 101 class. You should have learned the price of a commodity is based on its available quantity in relation to its current demand. If you weren't blessed to have taken Economics, all this means is that any increase in supply without a corresponding increase in demand will cause the price of the underlying commodity to decrease. This is because it gives the "demand" more options to choose from which drives prices of the individual units down as they compete against each other for selection. This is also why promotions aren't automatic after gaining rank within the dominance hierarchy. If your company is already fully staffed with managers, you will be considered excess supply and your price point will remain unchanged, even though your talents may warrant a higher value. Similar to a traffic jam, you will sit with your foot on the brakes until the excess is cleared and it's your turn to go.

But won't they just lay you off if you are in excess? Not if the business is operating under normal conditions without any singular event that radically alters their landscape overnight. Your company has a great amount invested in your development and wants to retain your abilities for when they are needed. Think of it as going into storage. While there, you will still be utilized, just not in a position that maximizes your full abilities. But not all will be ok with this. Some will become impatient and feel the corporation isn't giving them what's due. I will address this later in the chapter.

One thing to watch for in oversupply situations is the corporation will never directly tell you that you are in excess. This is by design—they don't want you knowing you could earn more elsewhere. They would rather keep you around for as long as possible, for as cheap as possible. For those who demand a raise anyways, endless excuses will be provided. Example—not meeting the minimum time requirement. If you're ever told this, which most employees inside a major corporation have, your bullshit meter should go bonkers, because, that's exactly what it is. *Bullshit.* But understand that no matter how ridiculous it sounds, your boss is only protecting the corporation against lawsuits. As in, if an employee who doesn't get a promotion claims it happened because they were discriminated against. The corporation can then fall back on its policy requiring employment for a certain amount of years to qualify, all while the person next to them is promoted after just months because of a "special circumstance" driven by an immediate one-time business need. Long story short, *it's all bullshit.* If the corporation needs to move somebody up or down they'll do so whenever they damn well please. They will also make sure their hands are kept clean while doing so should any grievances filed by the ever-constant herd of "shafted" employees.

That said, what must occur for supply to be lowered so you can move up and be paid what you are worth? A few things can trigger such an event. First, natural attrition.

People retire and someone is promoted to fill the retiree's spot. Someone further down is then promoted to fill the spot created by the person promoted into the retiree's position. This cycles all the way to the bottom until an open spot is created, eliminating the excess supply situation.

Another way supply is reduced is through a demand increase, creating an immediate need for more supply. Without going too deep into labor economics, all this means is a major event occurs which forces the recalibration of a company's labor demands to something other than what it had previously been operating under. For example, if a company suddenly doubles its business overnight, that would cause an immediate need for additional workers at all levels to satisfy the growth. But they could also *lose* half their business overnight, forcing them to abruptly reduce their workforce. Layoffs are common under such circumstances.

Oversupply situations are only one scenario that could occur after reaching the top of the dominance hierarchy. A corporation can also be in undersupply, sending an employee's demand through the roof. This will create a vacuum effect sending them up the ladder at incredible paces. To the untrained eye, this can be a confusing thing to witness. What most don't realize is that these people usually aren't anything special. They just rose to the top of their hierarchy at a time when the corporation was desperate for individuals with their skillset. This awarded them a significantly higher price point due to their extreme demand.

While ideal, undersupply situations aren't the norm. Most corporations pad their human capital requirements to protect against unplanned business needs. Acting as a safety net, this creates a thin but constant layer of oversupply within the ranks which must be waded through before it's your turn to climb.

The question then becomes what to do during this period. Do you just wait it out? That's one option. And for the non-aggressive types, this is the road most traveled as it's by far the least stressful path. But it comes with the risk that you could be sitting around for dubious amounts of time waiting for the tide to turn in your favor, something highly motivated individuals don't have the patience for.

The good thing is more options are available, one in particular being incredibly popular in today's times. *Pack up and leave.* You see, there's a beautiful truth about corporate supply & demand curves. *Every corporation has a different curve.* If the demand for your ability isn't high enough at your current company to warrant a promotion, there will certainly be others operating under different circumstances whose will. All you have to do is find them.

Enter social media. For the first time ever, business platforms like LinkedIn allow the world to bring together, at a macro level, both supply and demand for employees across the globe. Prior to LinkedIn, and the internet for that matter, this was done only by word of mouth which greatly limited the ability for corporations to staff appropriately. The result was significant under- and over-staffing issues within corporations, leading to extreme inefficiencies within their labor forces.

In today's world, things are much, much different. If there's an oversupply of a specific type of employee within a corporation, those employees can hop on LinkedIn and within minutes have access to hundreds of job postings from other corporations where their demand is much higher. This, my friends, is *revolutionary*. It's also why turnover rates at corporations are higher than ever. But some don't agree, citing the increased turnover stems from a reduced level of "company loyalty" from the younger generations. This couldn't be further from the truth. It stems from having access to better tools which didn't exist in previous generations—tools that give us exposure to opportunities which they were never able to see.

There could also be times when you are in undersupply and your company *still* isn't paying you an appropriate salary for your current demand. What do you do then? Many will seek a higher offer from another company and request their compensation be matched to that offer. This obviously wouldn't work in an oversupply situation as you're an easily replaceable asset and would be told not to let the door hit you on the way out. But when in undersupply, the corporation does NOT have this luxury and should be paying you as the scarce and valuable resource that you are. My opinion on this is simple. If you're working for a company where you must threaten them with another offer in order to be properly compensated, they are sending a clear signal that they don't have the best interest of their employees in mind. Will they match the other offer to keep you around? Maybe. But is it really necessary to go through all this in order to be paid what you are worth? Absolutely not. If they are not valuing you enough to compensate you appropriately, then you shouldn't value them enough to award them the benefit of your skills and experience. So once again, it's time to pack up and leave. Plus, there's always the chance they'll realize their mistake down the road, forcing them to offer you a return package you can't refuse. And believe me, it happens.

Up to this point, all we have talked about is either over- or under-supply situations in relation to demand and how such scenarios affect the price point your company awards you. But what if you're positioned at the intersection of supply and demand? In economics, it's called the equilibrium—where quantity of supply aligns with quantity of demand. Corporations refer to it as paying the "average market rate". It's here where you will neither be under- nor overpaid for your abilities and are expected to be fully content with your level of compensation.

But not all will be content with making the "average market rate". Fortunately, breaking out of the average isn't all that difficult. Just identify companies where anomalies exist within their labor force and hire on with them—specifically ones with the lowest supply as that will generate the highest demand and resultant price point. Consider it a form of arbitrage as seen in financial markets. But instead of exploiting price differentials on financial instruments, *you're exploiting price differentials on yourself.*

How exactly do you go about identifying these low supply, high demand companies? There are three main strategies, the first being the easiest. Do nothing and maintain positive relationships with coworkers who leave your company for better opportunities. If they impress their new employer, oftentimes they will be incentivized to reach back and recruit others to come along. This requires zero legwork on your part and is a very common thing to see happen within major corporations.

The second strategy is to always be interviewing with other companies, even if you have no intention of leaving your current employer. Two to three times a year is sufficient and can easily be done by keeping your LinkedIn profile current and applying to jobs as they appear on your homepage. LinkedIn does a magnificent job tailoring these opportunities towards your specific skills making it incredibly easy to see who's hiring in your area. You may realize after a couple of interviews that your price point is much higher outside of your current employer. If so, you will be presented with offers you can't refuse and will most likely leave for another job. It could also be that you're currently earning way above market, something you never would have known had you not been out interviewing. This will reinvigorate your enthusiasm for your current employer, leading to bigger and better opportunities should you just stay put.

*But you must continue interviewing.* Why? Because external labor markets can shift at a moment's notice. While your demand might not have been high enough during your initial interview to warrant a price point sufficient enough to leave your current employer, their business could later explode putting you in a much different position. It's during these times when having pre-established relationships with ten or fifteen different companies can be a very powerful tool. Most will retain your information and call you back when the demand for your services reaches a price you can't say no to.

The final technique for identifying low supply/high demand companies is without a doubt the most effective—form a relationship with every recruiter you can. This not only provides the broadest reach for potential opportunities but is the fastest and most direct. These individuals are paid on commission and seek out companies on your behalf. Setting them apart is their pre-established relationships with companies who notify them of available positions prior to releasing them into external labor markets, giving you a large head start when pursing the best opportunities. The best part is you don't have to find them. They find you. Every week, recruiters are out surfing LinkedIn profiles trying to find candidates to fill their clients' positions. Just keep your LinkedIn profile as robust as possible and you will have more inquiries than you know what to do with. But remember, you are not interested in their low hanging fruit. Make it clear you want companies who are in low supply so you can capitalize on their shortage, awarding you the highest price point. Fifty percent or more is not out of the question if you isolate a company with a true anomaly in their current labor supply. But most will end up with something much less after making this very common mistake. What mistake is that? *Telling the recruiter what your current salary is.*

While they will never disclose it, recruiters work for the hiring company whose goal is to pay you only enough to get you in the door and not a dollar more. This is why they ask what your current salary is because it gives the hiring company leverage when negotiating your offer. For example, if your external demand awards you a price point of $125k and the recruiter informs the hiring company that you are currently making $75k, they will try to manipulate your value by offering you something less than your true market value, but greater than your current salary. For example, $100k. The hiring company realizes most will not reject a thirty-three percent raise and hope you take the bait. If you accept, they just landed their dream candidate at a $25k discount.

How do you avoid making this mistake? First, when speaking with a recruiter and asked what you're currently making, you must flip the script. Tell them it's not what you're making that matters, but what you *could* make. Make it clear you are not interested in wasting your time for the standard twenty percent. You want companies with critical shortages who will offer the highest price point for your abilities. But for this to work, you must first know what that price point is. It can be easily calculated using sites like Glassdoor.com where corporate employees upload their compensation history. It's then consolidated and organized into a searchable format. Just look for the position you want and see what companies are paying for that job. For example, let's say I'm looking for a finance manager job in Atlanta. A quick search resulted in five hundred salaries ranging from $74k to $126k. Assuming I have the proper skills and experience to attain one of these positions, I would tell the recruiter my target salary is somewhere between $115-$125k. Even though there is technically no maximum that a company in a critical labor shortage will pay, requesting the top of the range found on Glassdoor should be a fair representation of this ceiling. Plus, it gives you actual data to validate your value if needed during salary negotiations.

However, constantly exploiting anomalies in your value has its drawbacks. It requires you to jump ship every so often, something which carries negative connotations in several ways. First, from an investment perspective. Bringing new employees into a corporation isn't cheap. It requires significant amounts of upfront capital in the form of administrative and training cost. For that investment to neutralize and eventually turn positive, new hires must provide back to the corporation several years of accumulated value via job productivity. If someone leaves their employer every six months, there is no way for this investment to ever materialize because the individual is never there long enough for it to do so. And once gone, the employer must write it off as a bad investment. Companies avoid this by scrutinizing potential red flags prior to investing in someone. A candidate with a history of company-jumping is one such flag. My recommendation is simple. Stay with your employer for a minimum of three years. I'm not saying there won't be unique circumstances which arise that force a move prior to this, but under normal circumstances it's a wonderful rule to live by. This gives your employer enough time to not only recoup their initial investment but to also receive a return should you perform properly. This reflects positively when searching for larger opportunities down the road. Why? Because it shows your next employer there's a high likelihood you'll do the same for them.

The second negative connotation associated with company-jumping is that it can be a sign of performance issues. Many times, people do it because they are continually chased out of companies after exhibiting poor performance, only to find another. Six months later their toxicity catches up to them again, creating yet another hostile situation. This forces them to start the cycle all over, adding more and more lines to their resume as they go. But the longer their resume gets, the less chance they have of continuing the appearance of being a quality employee. New employers will soon become wary and hesitate bringing them on board. Not only because their investment will likely be lost if they do, but because they can be burdened many times more when trying to get rid of them.

While many of these underperformers will leave without a fight, some will viciously attack. Improper termination suits are common and can cost hundreds of thousands, if not millions of dollars, to resolve. To protect themselves, most corporations will heavily document an employee's performance prior to firing them. Doing so lowers the risk of lawsuits by making it harder for a disgruntled employee to fabricate a story. But this isn't free either. Months of documentation is required which lowers productivity as managers become overburdened with non-value added paperwork.

In conclusion, go back and re-read the first paragraph. Picture yourself as the employee demanding a raise from your boss after accusing them of not recognizing your contributions to the corporation. Do you still believe that is a good idea? I sure hope not. By taking this approach, you're assuming they pay zero attention to what their employees are doing. The truth is they know exactly what you and your coworkers are doing. Why? Because it's their job. Managers at corporations have two responsibilities. First, to produce results. Second, to set up the next generation of leadership. Both have their own performance metrics tied to them. To assume they haven't noticed your contributions would be foolish. Maybe they have and just aren't impressed with what they see? It's time to take a step back, my friends. You might be the problem, not them.

What is my recommendation? Think about the dominance hierarchy and how it allows corporations to "test the goods" before deciding who to promote, greatly reducing their risk of making a bad choice. If you can't gain rank within it, you will never gain official rank within the corporation. Also think about everything covered regarding labor economics within corporations and how it affects salaries. Just because you gained rank within the dominance hierarchy doesn't mean you'll get promoted. The demand for you must also be present.

If you really want a promotion, don't accuse your boss of not paying attention to your performance. That will just irritate them. As stated in the last paragraph, always assume they are aware of your performance and where you rank within the dominance hierarchy. Then what should you do? Well, you must first assess whether you're actually at the rank within the hierarchy that you *think* you are. Odds are you aren't, which means it's you that needs the adjustment, not your boss. If this is the case, approach them with a solution that results in a win-win for both of you. Something along the lines of,

*"Mr. or Ms. Boss, I feel as if I have more to offer than what my current assignments are allowing for. I have high aspirations and will accept any project no matter the difficulty. I want to prove that I'm capable of achieving bigger and better things and will do whatever it takes to make that happen. Don't get me wrong, I would really like a promotion; but I want to earn it. All I ask is that you let me do just that. I will not let you down. Thank You."*

Let that soak in for a second. The goal here is to gain access to more difficult assignments. These will allow you the opportunity to prove yourself and climb higher within the hierarchy. Since your current assignments aren't getting you there, this is your only option. But as previously discussed, the demand must also be present. If it's not, you must wait it out or jump ship to another company with a higher demand. But should you jump, make sure to maintain good relationships with your current employer. You never know when you may need them again.

# V: THE CORPORATE CHAMELEON

THE LAST CHAPTER DISCUSSED THE corporate dominance hierarchy and how moving up within it is the determining factor behind who is and isn't promoted. There was zero mention of *how* it's actually done. In this chapter, we'll address just that. My friends, it's time to get down to business. Before we dive in, here are the three most important points in the book thus far.

*Important Point #1:*
*When you step foot inside a corporation,*
*you become an asset and will be treated as such.*

*Important Point #2:*
*All assets, including employees, have a shelf life.*
*As they expire, corporations must replace them on a*
*continual basis or risk going out of business. This gives*
*you an incredible amount of power as a new employee.*

*Important Point #3:*
*To be promoted, you must first gain rank within the domi-*
*nance hierarchy. Your timing must also align with the*
*corporation's demand for someone of your ability.*

But if the timing doesn't align, a gap between ones ranking within the dominance hierarchy and actual rank within the corporation is created. This results in employees not receiving the promotion they deserve and is the number one reason people leave for other companies. But as a new employee, you shouldn't yet be concerned with your actual ranking within the company. Don't put the cart in front of the horse. Focus on the dominance hierarchy first and deal with the rest after establishing rank within it. That said, for the rest of the book we're going to concentrate on just that—developing the specific skills necessary to quickly ascend through the dominance hierarchy so when promotions are handed out that you, and not your peers, are the one who receives them.

Think back to the last time you were on a busy interstate. You just left your house to go somewhere—work, bowling, cooking class, hot yoga, whatever. As soon as you pull onto the main highway, you are surrounded by hundreds of cars, all trying to reach their destination the quickest way possible. Some fly by you at one hundred miles per hour while others swerve in and out of your lane. You eventually make it to your exit, but not before having a near meltdown. Your heart is pounding and your emotions are boiled over. But you made it.

If you didn't pay attention to the other drivers, what would have happened? Odds are you would have crashed and never made it to your destination. But you did. Why? Because you were constantly adapting. You were changing speed, switching lanes, and moving left or right. You were defensive at times, offensive at others. It allowed you to survive.

Reaching your destination in a corporation is no different than driving on a busy highway. To make it in one piece without crashing, you must always be adapting to other peoples' "driving styles". Doing so will not only make you the most productive employee, but the most respected—the exact combination required to gain rank within the dominance hierarchy. This leads us to our next important point of the book thus far.

## *Important Point #4:*
### *Corporations Love Chameleons*

Chameleons? Yes, chameleons. In corporations, chameleons are the producers. Respected by all, they are capable of producing at extreme levels both as individuals and as leaders. Overcoming the most difficult obstacles with effortless ease, they are proof that fancy degrees and perfect GPA's will only take you so far inside the walls of a major corporation. But psychological adaptation is no easy skill to master. It requires patience, humility, and the ability to suck up your pride. But if properly executed, it can carry you further than all other skills *combined.*

And why is that? Because in corporations, you cannot produce unless you have the knowledge required to do so. In college, this knowledge was acquired from textbooks. Just study them and take an exam—that was how you "produced". This is no longer the case in a major corporation. Now confronted with projects and assignments that have real-life impacts on the profitability of a business, your ability to produce will be derived by your capacity to complete these assignments as accurately and efficiently as possible. But you will still need specific knowledge to do so—it just won't come from a textbook. Why? Because in the corporate world, there is no such thing. There are too many details involved with running a major corporation to fit them all in a single book. So where do employees turn to then? They turn to *people.*

In corporations, people are your textbook. Overflowing with knowledge from years of experience, they are the ones who will teach you everything required to be an effective producer. But unless you possess an incredibly fine-tuned set of people skills, accessing this knowledge will be impossible as the only way to unlock it is to first unlock the people who hold it. This is accomplished by crawling into their minds and making them believe that you're one in the same, regardless of how different you may actually be from them. Doing so will spawn feelings of trust and compassion, which when combined have the power to flatten even the strongest of defenses. You will then have unfettered access to their stores of corporate knowledge that can be used to accomplish your assignments both faster and better, making you not only the most productive person in your employee class, but the most respected as well. And as previously mentioned, these are the key ingredients necessary for establishing rank within the dominance hierarchy.

But what is it about adaptation that makes others respect you? Because corporations are full of narcissistic demanding assholes who believe the world revolves around them and them only. These individuals spend their days beating on others to attain what they need while caring only about themselves and their own personal interests. After years of abuse, the recipients of this behavior become emotional robots with one setting—cold. So, when someone is able to put their personal preferences aside and engage with them in a way that makes *them* feel comfortable, it makes them think— hey, that person made me feel good, I respect that. It's at this precise moment when they will unlock their brain and give you untethered access to their knowledge. It's also when you are awarded the power of influence over them. And as discussed back in chapter three, corporations salivate over employees who can demonstrate such an ability. They are well aware that production levels skyrocket when individuals are led by people they naturally want to follow.

To be successful in a major corporation, you don't have to know everything about your company, you just have to know the people who know everything. And, you must retain open access to their knowledge at all times. Think about it this way. Let's go back to the college textbook. Whenever you needed information, you turned to the necessary chapter and studied it. In a corporation, you will still turn to the necessary chapter, it will just be a person and not a page number. That said, your coworkers should never again be thought of as just coworkers. Rather, as different chapters in the textbook, each whom carries specific knowledge regarding different areas of the business. When you need something, just turn to the right person and gather what you need.

Sounds simple, right? Multiple times in this book I have stated that only one person gives a damn about you inside a corporation. That person is you. Do you really think someone focused on their own success is going to be all that enthusiastic about helping you out with yours? Outperforming them will only hinder their own progression. That said, the answer isn't just no, but hell no they won't be forthcoming when providing what you need. Will they do it just because they know they'll get in trouble with a higher authority should they not? Probably. But that isn't the level of responsiveness we're looking for. While you may still get the data, it won't be timely and what you do receive will be a stripped-down version. What you need is complete, accurate, and timely responses and the only way to get them is to approach your coworkers in a way that makes *them* feel comfortable, not you.

Too many times have I witnessed fellow employees end up in catastrophic collisions because they refused to adapt. Whether through email or in person, they would engage only on their psychological terms. This led to emotions boiling over when their inability to "unlock" their coworkers restricted the flow of information required to complete their assignments. With their relationships now totaled, never again were they able to access the knowledge of these individuals. The next time they approached them for help, they were met with this very candid response— "I'm sorry, I don't have time right now". In the corporate world, this is the equivalent of "eat shit, buddy". A significant drop-off in their performance resulted as they forever lost access to those individuals chapters in the corporate textbook.

I'm now going to break down the two most difficult personality types that you'll encounter in a major corporation. You will certainly come across more personalities. But these are by far the most common when it comes to challenging people. If you can master these, you can master anything.

### Personality Type #1: *The Arrogant Asshole*

There is no corporation on Earth that doesn't have their fair share of arrogant assholes. Prancing around as if no one else exists, they pride themselves on being the smartest person in the room, though many times are far from it. Cold and unapproachable, they can be incredibly intimidating to newcomers, especially those not yet indoctrinated into the brutal world of corporate survivalism. But like a rash that never goes away, these individuals require constant surveillance and should never be ignored. Why? Because in a corporation, your success is based upon your ability to not only work with people you like, but also ones you don't.

A mistake many individuals make in large corporations is believing they can rely only on people they "click with" to get what they need. What they fail to realize is how much knowledge is left on the table by doing so. But unlocking knowledge held by people your complete and total opposite is no easy task. Extreme humility is required as personal preferences must be thrust aside in exchange for uncomfortable norms established by those whose knowledge you so desperately seek. That said, there is no personality that will require more of your humility than an arrogant asshole. In order to successfully unlock their chapter in the corporate textbook, you must bury your pride and "submit" to their dominance. Why? Because arrogant assholes don't play well with other arrogant assholes. They want complete and total control with nobody challenging their ego. Attempting to knock them off this psychological pedestal will cause a collision and forever limit your access to their chapter in the corporate textbook.

If you can't challenge them, how do you get what you need? You *fool* them by making them feel guilty about not helping you. This requires you to beat them at their own game and is no different than how you go about dealing with a mean cat. When it comes to mean cats, the more you challenge it, the harder it will bite. But if you sit back and pretend it doesn't exist, it will eventually be on your lap looking for a scratch. The same goes for arrogant assholes inside corporations. When you need something, politely submit your request and let them know you're in need. Then, run like hell and leave the rest up to them. By doing so you're ensuring the request remains within their control and on their timeline, both which are critical pieces that must be satisfied in order to get a response. Applying pressure will do nothing but make them feel as if they are losing control, leaving you empty-handed.

You may be thinking you can't wait around forever. While that may be true, don't take the bait and confront them about it. You're only wasting your time. If they want to drag it out, they will. This plays right into your hands. Why? Because there will always be another person who shares similar knowledge that can help. You just have to figure out who they are. And, once the asshole realizes you moved on without asking them a second time, they'll feel abandoned, at which point they'll come running back to you faster than you could ever imagine. The battle is now won. You beat them at their own game and your access to their chapter in the corporate textbook will now be forever available if ever needed again.

## Personality Type #2: *The Job Protector*

In major corporations, there's only one personality more difficult than the arrogant assholes—the employees who've built up significant salaries after twenty or thirty years with the company and are terrified of losing their job to younger, cheaper employees. But unlike arrogant assholes who have fairly easy workarounds to get what you need, accessing knowledge from a job protector can be an extremely difficult chore. Why? Because you are no longer dealing with minor psychological issues. Rather, it's now *survival* issues at play. This, my friends, is a whole new ballgame. And, if you don't handle these people with extreme care, it will cost you dearly as they carry significant amounts of corporate knowledge that you must absolutely establish and retain access to.

That said, here's the kicker. As a new employee, guess who'll be training you? It won't be your manager. They will be busy with larger, more important items. It's dumped on the people with years of experience who have both the knowledge and the time to train you—usually the job protectors. To the corporation, this is a match made in heaven. They are pairing you with a seriously experienced person that's going to teach you everything you need to know about the business. But remember, these individuals have been around for long enough that by this point they are being paid extremely well. You, on the other hand, are at the bottom of the scale making a fraction of what they do. Now, put yourself in their shoes. How would you feel if the corporation instructed you to teach everything you knew to an employee making one-third your salary? Think about it. When you're finished training them, the corporation will then have two equally skilled employees, one costing much less than the other. Fast forward six months. The business hits a rough patch and layoffs are announced. Who do you think they'll look at first? The employees making the lowest amount or the ones making the highest? If someone can do the same job for less cost, the highest wage earner gets laid off. Simple as that.

But make no mistake. These high-salaried employees have been around the block a few times in their years. They've seen this happen time and time again and are fully aware that training a younger, cheaper employee may very well be the last thing they do for the corporation. Because of this, some will make it as painful as possible. It's no different than giving a cat a bath. It will eventually get done, but the process of getting there is nothing short of a world war.

Training aspect aside, you will need these people just as much if not more than any other class of employee within the corporation. Why? Because they hold the keys to some of the most confidential and sought-after chapters in the entire corporate textbook. But to gain access, you must implement a significantly different technique than what is used for the arrogant assholes. Instead of being submissive and non-confrontational to avoid challenging their ego, you must now act in ways that calm their fears regarding job security. And just how is that done? By finding and triggering their inner "parent" so they no longer see you as a young, cheap employee, but rather as one of their own kids. This will activate the powerful emotions of love, trust, and empathy, which when combined places you on an emotional level matched only by one other group of people—their own children. You will then be granted all the same benefits including guidance, assistance, and protection, along with anything else required for you to succeed. This is accomplished by showing the same love and respect you would to your own mom or dad and hope it penetrates their shell. If successful, their natural instincts will take over. From that point on you will be well taken care of.

Let's face it. There's no human on Earth that can stand strong in the face of love. We all melt. Even the biggest assholes turn into soft piles of mush when somebody knows how to push their buttons. The key is figuring out just what those buttons are and learning when to push them. But you must be careful—you can only push them so many times. As with anything in life, moderation is key. It's just like eating tacos. They are amazing at first. But if you eat them ten days in a row you'll quickly get burned out. Pushing somebody's "button" is no different. You must use it sparingly and allow the demand for your love to build back up before you hit it again. Otherwise, the person will realize what you're doing and all trust will be lost, putting you in a worse spot than you were in to begin with.

To help illustrate, I'll use an example from my own experience. It was around the fourth year of my career when the corporation mandated that I be trained in financial planning, a prerequisite for my specific career path. In my company, this was a tightly held group as the data managed within it was extremely sensitive. Any errors committed were immediately exposed at the highest levels of the corporation. This made it a particularly selective process for whom the corporation allowed into the group. That said, I have no clue how I became that person. I guess I was a little too good at my own game (adapt, adapt, adapt).

The financial planning team was run by a lady named Cindy (I am using fake names for the purposes of this example). She was smart, experienced, and *fiercely* protective of her turf. By far the most territorial person in the office, she possessed specialized knowledge that nobody else in the building had. In a corporation, this is job security at its finest. And, she was determined to make sure it remained that way. She knew that transferring her knowledge to another employee would diminish her value and make her replaceable. But on the other hand, the corporation realized they would be in big trouble if something ever happened to her. It was then when my journey with Ms. Cindy began.

At first, things were a bit rough. I was like a dog sniffing around the dinner table for scraps. On good days, Ms. Cindy would kindly brush something off her plate for me to gobble up. But those days were few and far between. For the most part, all I received was a brief pat on the head followed by a shooing back to my corner. After all, she was keenly aware of what the corporation could do with her after I was fully trained and she was not about to take the bait.

I was stuck between a rock and a hard place. My future success within the corporation relied on attaining full and complete access to her "chapter". However, she was in complete control of just what knowledge she would and would not pass down to me. And, she wasn't about to give me anything more than what the corporation required of her. This posed a major problem for me. I needed *all* of her knowledge, not just pieces. But to get it, I had to find her secret button; the one that would leave her defenses crumbled and powerless should I ever push it. This would require me to "adapt" at the highest levels and would later prove to be the greatest conquest of my entire career.

Enter peanut butter. Yes, peanut butter. As the weeks passed by, I began noticing that Ms. Cindy had a passion for peanut butter. And by passion, I mean she damn near put it on everything. Bananas, candy, pizza, ice cream, you name it. She believed that no matter how much you ate, it was good for you. I adamantly disagreed and thought it should only be eaten in small portions as the fat and sugar contents were extremely high. That being said, our relationship at the time was fairly wide open. We discussed anything and everything. So, I walked into her office one day to properly "educate" her on its nutritional value. Unfortunately for me, I had yet to learn one very important lesson in life. Don't *ever* confront a female about her eating habits. As I was in the middle of explaining why too much peanut butter was bad, I quickly realized I had stepped into extremely dangerous territory. I tried to change the dialogue, but it was too late. I didn't even get the chance for a closing argument. I ran out of her office fearing for my life. It was the most scared I have ever been of a female and is a lesson I will never forget.

You may be asking, didn't that shut down all access to her knowledge? Yes—she hardly said a word to me for about a month. But Christmas was fast approaching and I knew that females of all ages loved presents. This was a golden opportunity to heal the wound and re-open my access to her brain. But what would I get her? Peanut butter, of course. But I couldn't just get her a jar of it. I needed to go big. So, I went to a large grocery store and bought every single peanut butter-related item they had. You wouldn't believe how much stuff is peanut butter-flavored. I ended up purchasing over thirty items and stuffed them into the largest box I could find, wrapped it with a big bow, and left it on her front porch. Later that night, she opened the present and sent me a picture of her entire family surrounded by all the peanut butter items. I had made her holiday.

Needless to say, that was a game-changer. Not only was I able to re-establish access to her knowledge, but could do so at levels previously unachieved. Anything I ever wanted was now within arm's reach and I never had to beg for scraps again. I had found her button and cracked her defenses, defenses which remain immobilized to this current day.

Hopefully you now understand the importance adapting your psychological approach in order to gain access to your coworker's chapters in the corporate textbook. Without it, you'll certainly struggle when completing assignments and will most certainly fail at your job.

But this is only the first step in your corporate chameleon life. You must also adapt the *psychological delivery* of your finished assignments to fit your boss's "eye". This step is much easier given you only have one person to figure out unlike before where tens if not hundreds of coworkers are involved. But you must be careful—the repercussions of screwing up here are exponentially higher. Remember, your boss is the one responsible for your performance reviews, not your coworkers. You must be incredibly cautious before presenting a finished assignment to them. If they can't interpret what you submit, it can be just as detrimental to your career as failing to complete it in the first place.

Before we go further, let me address one of the biggest fallacies you will encounter in the workplace—how to become a "favorite". The common belief is that in order to become one, you must permanently attach your lips to the boss's ass. While true in some places, this type of behavior usually gets you nowhere. The individuals who partake in these activities generally aren't the brightest and fool themselves into believing it will accelerate them further than simply focusing on their work assignments. Let me be very clear. Engaging in this behavior will never take the place of real work. Do not ever think that kissing someone's ass will put you on a faster track for a promotion than the next person. All it does is communicate to the corporation that you're incompetent and lack the ability to offer any real value, making the behavior do the exact opposite of what it was intended it to do in the first place.

At the end of the day, bosses like employees who get things done because it makes their lives easier. If you're in their office three hours a day refilling their coffee, they'll quickly realize you're a non-producer who's only going to hold them back as a manager. And furthermore, ass-kissers lose the respect of their coworkers—they are viewed as trying to circumvent the system. Remember, your coworkers are the ones holding the keys to the "corporate textbook". You cannot afford to have your access to their chapters shut down. If you're going to kiss anybody's ass, it should be theirs, not your bosses. Instead of filling your boss's coffee cup, take the pot around and ask your coworkers if they would like a refill. You will be blown away by how much these small deeds increase your job performance.

So, if ass-kissing isn't how you become a favorite, how do you become one? *By delivering completed assignments of the highest quality and in ways your boss can easily interpret.* Too many times have I seen fellow employees spend vast amounts of time working on projects only to have them end up in the trashcan because they weren't delivered properly. Ample substance aside, their failure to properly identify their bosses' preferences and adapt their delivery to fit within those parameters made their submissions all but worthless. Bosses are busy enough as it is—they are not going to waste their time decoding an employee's work just to figure out what it means. They are highly stressed and will move to another employee until they find someone who can get them what they want and how they want to see it.

Let's look at this from another angle. Think about the last time you drove through a burger joint and had your order screwed up. For me, I always get heavy mustard and extra pickles. You would think it was rocket science given the number of times they get it wrong. To make things worse, I'm usually miles down the road before I realize it's incorrect. What do I end up doing? I either turn around and get it fixed or I accept it and carry on with my day. Either way, it sours my mood. Never again will I visit that location.

What does this have to do with adapting your work

products? Imagine yourself as the burger joint and your boss the customer in the drive-through. Let's say he or she asks for a burger with extra mustard and pickles and you deliver one with extra ketchup and onions. Even though you still delivered them an excellent burger, *it's not how they wanted it.* And, it doesn't matter if every other boss in the corporation likes theirs with ketchup and onions. They are not *your* boss. Your boss likes mustard and pickles. You must always deliver that perfect burger. This, my friends, is how you become a favorite.

But what happens if you keep screwing up your boss's burger? Think about it this way. Say you and a fellow employee had been tasked to complete the same assignment for your boss. When it came time to deliver, you submitted a massive excel spreadsheet with all the answers on it. You did so because your prior boss loved to see data this way and assumed it would be acceptable with your new boss as well. Your coworker took a different route. They had been paying attention to how your boss responded to other employee's assignments and discovered he or she likes to see data in high-level summaries with the excel sheets only as backup. They also recognized the new boss's preference to have those summaries put onto pretty PowerPoint slides with perfect alignment, consistent font, and the company colors already as the background. This prevents them from having to spend time dinking with formatting issues prior to sending it up the chain. With this knowledge, your coworker formats and submits their assignment accordingly.

Over the next few weeks you begin to notice something very odd. Your boss begins to shift all the larger, higher visibility projects to your coworker. They are assigned the "prize" projects while you are given the low-hanging fruit. You scratch your head, wondering where you went wrong. I'll tell you where you went wrong. You delivered a ketchup and onion burger when they wanted mustard and pickles! Your coworker figured this out ahead of time and delivered them a perfect mustard and pickle burger on the first try. As a result, your boss now turns to them when something important needs to get done and will continue to do so for as long as they keep receiving those perfect burgers. If your favorite restaurant screwed your order up ten times in a row, would you continue to go there? Or, would you start going to their competitor down the road who gets it right every time?

I'll close with this. The only difference between a burger joint and a corporate employee is that your customer (i.e. your boss) won't tell you how they want their burger. This is up to you to figure out. But how do you do that? You watch them like a hawk, unraveling their psychological makeup and pinpointing how they like to see data. It may take some time, but once you crack the code you will forever become their favorite for as long as you're under their chain of command.

# VI: THE BATTLE BEGINS – LET YOUR ARMY DO THE DIRTY WORK

WE'RE NOW THROUGH THE TOUGHEST part of the book where I covered everything from the importance of the corporate ski lift to how maintaining continuous access to your coworkers' chapters in the corporate textbook is the key to making your way up the dominance hierarchy (adapt...adapt...adapt...). Let's now discuss how to deal with the *opposition*.

When looking at the hierarchical structure of corporations, there's a common thread between them all. The higher you rise, the stiffer the competition becomes as the number of available positions begins to decrease. Given the scarcity of such positions, some will become bitter as you accelerate past of them in terms of job performance. Unable to act responsibly when things don't go their way, these individuals will transform from a friendly coworker to your worst nightmare in a matter of seconds. In little league, they are the ones who threw their bat after striking out, crying and screaming while placing blame on everyone other than themselves. Their behavior in corporations twenty-five years later is no different. They still react in the same dramatic ways, especially when confronted with situations where employees of equal footing are out-pacing them in terms of career advancement. And once behind, they will do whatever it takes to regain their footing, even if that means playing dirty.

In chapter four, I stated prisoners and corporate employees have more in common than you think. Both can either submit to higher ranking individuals within their respective dominance hierarchies or overthrow them to become the dominant figure. In prisons, this is accomplished through physical brutality. These behaviors obviously won't fly in a corporation, forcing employees to use their minds instead of their fists. Either way, the end result is the same—a potential change to one's rank within the hierarchy.

But as mentioned, not everyone will play by the rules. Instead of out-smarting or out-working you, some will use deceitful tactics to avoid challenging you directly knowing they cannot be beat you fair and square. One such tactic is launching an assault against your reputation to harm your credibility. Should they succeed, you will be sent tumbling down the rankings leaving them with an easier, less obstructed pathway up. Little do they know these attacks rarely succeed and almost always boomerang back around causing significant damage upon their own careers for reasons I will soon explain.

But why go after your reputation? Because it's by far the most influential yet vulnerable asset you have in a major corporation. Every decision ever made regarding your career advancement will be based upon it. Think of it as your personal glass house, one you continually build upon as the years pass. To quote Warren Buffet, "It takes twenty years to build a reputation and five seconds to destroy it". This means your entire glass house can be shattered in the blink of an eye. This can be triggered by one of two things. A self-inflicted wound resulting from your own actions, or, because it was hit by an enemy rock. *One person, one rock.* That's all it takes. And guess what? The nicer your glass house, the more vulnerable it becomes as more and more will be threatened by its presence.

Before we dive into how to protect your reputation from such attacks, let's first discuss how corporations use reputations and why they are so vital to your success within one. As discussed, to be promoted within a major corporation, you must rise to the top of the dominance hierarchy and hope the timing of your ascent aligns with the corporation's demand for someone of your abilities. If they do, you can all but guarantee yourself that big promotion. But for the dominance hierarchy to be an effective tool, corporations must first identify where their employees rank within it. The problem is there isn't a tangible list that shows them these rankings. So where do they look? They look at their employees' *reputations.*

Reputations are a corporation's "invisible list" that shows where each employee ranks within the dominance hierarchy. And, the relative strength of each (or lack thereof) is based off an employee's cumulative average rating similar to what you'd see on Amazon or Yelp. But instead of being determined by what someone thought of a specific product or service, these ratings are now derived from an employee's interactions throughout the corporation. Nevertheless, the principal remains the same. To be at the top of the list, your average must be higher than everyone else's.

To help illustrate, consider the Mexican food industry. For anybody who's ever traveled to my hometown of Houston, you quickly learn that Mexican food is a big deal there. At any given location there are twenty different Mexican restaurants within a three-mile radius. Needless to say, I've certainly eaten my fair share. Some good, some bad, some *really* bad. But when I was growing up, we didn't have Yelp to guide us along. This made trying somewhere we had not yet been a risky adventure. If we were lucky, we knew someone who had tried it and could ask for an opinion. If not, we were left with the oldest trick in the book—counting the cars in the parking lot. The higher the count, the better the food. Although not as foolproof as Yelp ratings, it certainly allowed for some degree of confidence when eating blind.

After Yelp came along, we never had to count cars again. A quick search on the website allowed us to view the most reputable restaurants we had not yet tried. But what does this have to do with corporations? In corporations, this same type of review and selection process also occurs. It's just executives searching for the best employees to promote instead of hungry people looking for Mexican food. But like Mexican food, these executives cannot waste their time and money on a bad selection. Doing so could hinder the corporation's performance. To mitigate this risk, corporations base their advancement decisions on employee reputations as they are by far the most reliable source of data they have. This is precisely why building a solid reputation (and protecting it) inside a major corporation is absolutely critical for your success.

You might be thinking this is nonsense and that there's no such thing as a decentralized rating system in corporations as there is on Yelp. Believing this is a huge mistake that can have catastrophic consequences for your career. When people believe this, they tend not to put as much effort into their interactions with lower level employees as they mistakenly believe they are powerless and cannot affect the progression of their careers. What they fail to realize is these people *are* in positions of power, it's just their power isn't as obvious as that which is carried by actual managers within the corporation. In reality, they actually have more power as they are responsible for the bulk of your reviews. Remember, when it comes to your overall average, a review is a review. Neglecting interactions with lower level employees will affect your average just as much as neglecting them with higher ranking ones. It would be like saying certain Yelp reviews hold no weight because the reviewer wasn't a professional food critic.

But shouldn't a positive assessment from a higher-ranking employee have a greater impact on your career? At the end of the day, yes. However, you must understand the process from which that assessment is derived. Given their positions, they oftentimes are not able to spend enough time with lower-ranking employees to form an honest opinion and will base their valuation on what the rest of the corporation is saying about that person (i.e. they piggyback off of your coworkers). This is precisely why those lower level reviews are so critical as they not only feed into your overall average but also serve as the foundational support higher-level executives need to officially endorse someone.

Now that we understand what reputations are used for, lets discuss the mechanics behind how they are actually formed. The first step is that every review must be communicated across the corporation. These reviews serve as the ingredients which reputations are built upon and must be readily available so that every employee's "average score" and resultant reputation strength can easily be calculated throughout the general population. But how are they communicated? There isn't a "Yelp" within corporations for employees to post them to. As it turns out, one's not needed. Employees *love* to talk, especially about other employees—the good, the bad, and everybody's favorite, the ugly. Therefore, a website isn't necessary as these reviews are immediately absorbed throughout the corporation as soon as they enter the office atmosphere.

I have now covered what reputations are made from, what they are used for, and the process from which they are created. Let's now discuss how to protect them. In the beginning of the chapter, I stated the better your reputation, the more attention it will attract from envious coworkers. This will lead some to directly challenge you an attempt to overtake your ranking. However, there will be others who won't be so forthcoming and will instead rely on deceitful tactics to unseat you. The most common being to smear your reputation by spreading "fake reviews" in an attempt lower your average rating and overall position within the hierarchy. But as dishonest as that may be, protecting your reputation against such attacks is actually easier than you think. Let me explain.

During the early stages of my career, I moved to Atlanta from Ft. Worth as part of a leadership training program where I quickly established myself as a go-to employee. That said, I noticed certain individuals weren't as amused with my ascent through the ranks as I was. Given the limited number of management slots to go around, they viewed me as a threat to their own well-being and proceeded to do everything they could to derail me, regardless of whether or not they even knew me. Keep in mind I had beaten them fair and square. I outworked them, outsmarted them, and outwitted them. But as discussed earlier, people in the corporate world care about one thing–themselves. This was something I was about to experience first-hand.

Before I knew it, my reputation was under serious assault. Everything from rumors about my sexuality to being an alcoholic. There was one individual in particular who felt overly threatened and took direct aim at me. He hurled rock after rock at my reputation in an attempt to neutralize my climb through the ranks. Nothing was off the table—from spreading the aforementioned rumors to discrediting my work products every chance he could get. Talk about a wakeup call!

I knew the assault had to be stopped before irreversible damage was done. But how? The "prisoner" in me wanted to go knock his teeth out, albeit at the expense of my job. This obviously wasn't an option. I therefore took a passive stance with hopes it would resolve itself naturally. After a few more months without resolution, my frustration eventually reached a breaking point. Something had to be done. And as it turned out, something was already being done. I just didn't know about it.

You see, the people this person was spreading lies to weren't just any regular employees. They were individuals I had spent years building solid relationships with. I didn't know it, but they had been fighting back on my behalf the entire time. Anytime one of his falsehoods would float to the surface, my people would immediately rise up and shoot it out of the water, sending its shattered remains back to the shadowy depths from which it came from. Sometimes it was immediate, other times it would take a while. Either way, the result was always the same— its complete and total destruction prior to it having any significant impact upon my career.

This experience taught me one of the most powerful lessons I ever learned about working inside large corporations. Don't waste your time and energy getting worked up over someone coming after your reputation. The relationships formed with coworkers via the adaptation methods previously discussed will create a "psychological barrier" surrounding it on all sides, keeping rock-throwers far enough out that they cannot reach it with their throws. I didn't realize it, but this had been saving my reputation all along. No matter how hard he tried, he couldn't hit me. My supporters wouldn't allow for it. He was eventually forced to give up. I defeated his attacks and never lifted a finger. In other words, *I let my army do the dirty work.*

Building an army big enough to fully surround your reputation is no easy task. It can take many years. But it's certainly possible and is accomplished using a skill we've already covered in this book—adapt...adapt...adapt. This is because when you put yourself on someone else's playing field, that person will provide you the same benefits as someone they have close personal ties to—support, compassion, and, most importantly, *protection*. This is why adaptation is so important. It not only enables you to attain the information you need from the corporate textbook but also serves as the main building block for the construction of your "fence". However, not all fences are created equal. Just like anything else in life, you get out what you put in. Invest heavily in your interactions with others and you'll be left with a fortress that will repel any attack regardless of size or strength. Decide not to prioritize your relationships and be left with nothing more than a rotted-out shell that will allow even the smallest of invaders to walk right through.

We've now covered the four most important aspects of reputations—what they are used for, what they are made of, how they are formed, and how to protect them. Before we close this chapter, I have four additional facts about reputations that I would like to cover.

### Random Fact #1:
*When someone gives you a positive review,*
*they are endorsing themselves just as much as they are you.*

When you are given an endorsement, the endorser is telling the world that you are a great employee. They could be perfectly correct in their assessment. They could also be perfectly incorrect. If the latter is true, it's not only an issue for you the endorsee, but for the endorser as well. Why? Because they will be seen as someone who lacks solid judgment. This leads people to protect their endorsements to the bitter end, regardless of whether their assessment is correct or not.

Take hiring managers for example. This is a major responsibility given the individuals they bring into the company will someday form the underlying current responsible for powering the corporation forward. But if they are unable to correctly estimate the talent levels of employment candidates, not only will they put the corporation at risk by hiring incompetent employees, but their career as a manager as well. This is why you'll never hear a hiring manager admit they hired a dud. It's career suicide. They will fight for these people until the very end, regardless of how worthless they turn out to be.

Hiring managers aren't the only people who fight to protect their endorsees for reasons other than what drove their endorsement in the first place. Ordinary employees will put up a fight as well. But not because they fear losing their job. Rather, because they don't want to be proven wrong. With their pride at stake, these individuals will aggressively defend their endorsees when attacked, even if deserved. Until they officially pull their support, they'll continue protecting them tooth and nail as their pride is as closely attached to that employee's reputation as the employee themselves.

But everyone has their limits. Should an endorsee continue to fall short of expectations, the endorser will eventually be forced to cut ties or risk being dragged down with them. A difficult situation to face, especially when friendships are involved. If ever faced with this scenario, you must not be timid. Remember, you are working for a reason—to put food on your table and clothes on your family's backs. You must immediately un-link yourself from the falling anchor as its weight will eventually become so great that you can no longer support it without taking on water yourself. Think of it as riding in a canoe. Taking on a small amount of water will have little effect. It's when the amount becomes great enough to disrupt the canoe's counterbalance that it becomes dangerous.

While issuing one or two bad endorsements may not affect you, having a string of them could be seen by the corporation as a symptom of a much deeper issue—your inability to properly assess the value someone can provide to the corporation. You must therefore practice maximum restraint when giving endorsements as you only have so much leeway before your own reputation begins to suffer. But if they are so dangerous, why even make them? Because having a history of identifying top talent will assist you in landing higher salaried positions where you can exercise those talents for the greater good of the corporation. If a pattern arises of continually issuing bad endorsements, you could permanently disqualify yourself from such positions. You can however hedge your risk. The most popular technique being to only endorse someone whom already has numerous endorsements from other people of stature within the corporation. Doing so creates an insurance policy. Should they end up a dud, you can dilute the failed endorsement across multiple others who also endorsed them. This will prevent you from taking all the punishment yourself.

Random Fact #2:
*Reputations are compounding.*

Remember when we discussed how salaries work like compounding interest? Reputations are no different. One positive review plus one positive review doesn't equal two positive reviews. A bandwagon effect takes place where three, four, or even five positive reviews may result. It's no different than a snowball rolling down a mountain. With each new rotation, its surface area becomes larger and larger allowing it to grow exponentially as it continues down.

But how can this be? I mean, people won't endorse you without even knowing you, will they? The truth is others will endorse you when it serves them best. It's a beautiful thing to experience, especially if you're on the receiving end, accumulating positive reviews from not only people you've interacted with, but also ones you haven't. Here's why this happens. As your reputation "rolls down the mountain", it will eventually hit a certain size, weight, and speed that attempting to stop would be a death trap for anyone who may try. This is because the momentum behind your snowball (i.e. your army of supporters) will eventually become so great that only a significant force could stop it, a force which most employees don't possess. This leaves any employee not already part of the movement one of two choices. Get crushed or jump on the bandwagon and go along for the ride like everyone else (i.e. give you their endorsement). In reputation terms, this is what I call the bliss point—the point when you can do absolutely nothing and still have your reputation flourish and grow, feeding on itself rather than relying on an influx of new reviews. And how do you reach this stage? Be aware of your surroundings and adapt as necessary to attain solid reviews from every person you interact with. If you're successful at this, your reputation will eventually hit this tipping point, allowing it to power itself naturally without any further input on your part.

Random Fact #3:
*Other employees' reputations can be just as valuable*
*to you as they are to the corporation itself.*

Let's think back to the definition of the dominance hierarchy. Within it, there's a section that reads,

*"But rather than compete each time they meet, relative relationships are formed between each member of the group. This leads to the creation of a professional order that is subject to change each time a dominant employee is challenged by a subordinate one."*

As you may have noticed, there's a section in bold. There will never be a time while resting upon the top of the hierarchy when you won't be under constant attack from subordinate ranking members. It's basic human nature for them to want your spot. To protect your ranking, you must know who's rising below you. This allows you to prepare for their challenge ahead of time. You do this by keeping tabs on everyone's reputation to see where each employee ranks within the hierarchy, just as the corporation does. But unlike the corporation who uses this information to identify who to promote, you will use it to monitor those encroaching upon your status, allowing you to recalibrate your own personal performance as necessary in order to maintain your ranking. It's no different than being in prison. If someone wants to take you out, you'll obviously want to know about it ahead of time so you can adjust your behavior as necessary. Doing so will make an overthrow attempt extremely difficult for anyone who may try.

There will certainly be times of smooth sailing when there are no such challengers. But this is where the danger lies. There are many who've become overly complacent only to be sent tumbling back down the rankings after being caught off-guard by other, more aggressive employees. But had they been listening to the "buzz on the street", they would have identified these opponents long beforehand, allowing them to amend their performance back to competition levels prior of their arrival. Winning a fight becomes inherently easier if you know both when and where the punch will be coming from prior to it ever being thrown.

Random Fact #4:
*Your resume isn't worth a penny more
than the paper it's written on.*

But, but, shouldn't your resume be more important than your reputation when deciding how "valuable" you are to the corporation? No. And here's why. Let's think back to Mexican restaurants. What's the first thing you do after taking your seat? Most will sprinkle the chips with a little salt and crack the menu open to see what looks good. Say you decide on the combination number twelve dinner—one beef burrito smothered with mole sauce and a side of rice and beans. But before you order, your friend tells you that one of their friends told them the beef burrito was terrible. Where does that leave you? If you're like any other person you'd play it safe and order the crunchy taco plate. Think about what just happened. You hadn't even tasted the beef burrito yet, however, a friend of a friend said they didn't like it. This was enough to sway your decision, even though the picture on the menu looked delicious.

In corporations, resumes work the same way. While fun to look at, they normally aren't the deciding factor when determining who does and doesn't get promoted. Could there be items on the "menu" which look mouth-watering good? Sure. But in the corporate world, as with Mexican food, placing an order based exclusively off the way something looks can be risky. This is why corporations will never rely entirely on a resume itself, but rather what others are *saying* about the person. This greatly reduces their risk of making the wrong selection.

To summarize, reputations are what management uses to hedge their risk when selecting who to promote into positions of power. They want the best of the best in these slots as they'll be responsible for driving a higher bottom line while also reducing the corporation's risk for achieving those returns. Hence, it's critical to not only establish a solid reputation through positive reviews from your coworkers but to also ensure its everlasting protection by maintaining those relationships should it ever come under assault.

# VII: CLOTHING - YES, AN ENTIRE CHAPTER

SUSTAINING A FULL-TIME JOB INSIDE a major corporation is no easy task. You must adhere to a boss's instructions, abide by the corporation's rules and put in plenty of "extra hours" so you're not mistaken for a loafer. But as depressing as that may sound, it's not all that bad. Most of the rules you encounter have a defined purpose and were established to promote a higher bottom line for the corporation. There are actually some pretty good ones out there. What about the one that says you have to show up for work? I mean, that's a pretty good rule. Or the one that says you can't look at sexy pictures on the internet all day? Also a good rule. These are as cut and dry as it gets, and you will certainly be fired should you break either one of them.

But what about the dress code? That's a rule, isn't it? Absolutely. Odds are your new company will fall into one of two categories—business professional or business casual. Regardless of where your company resides, proper clothing choices will undoubtably be one of the most complex psychological battlegrounds you will ever encounter. But if played correctly, it can propel you to the highest levels possible.

The rest of the chapter will focus on two keep principles. There isn't a corporation on this planet where these two things are not true.

## Principle #1:
### *Clothing Opens Doors*

If you've ever sold anything online, you know it takes a little work. No matter how great your product is, it won't sell unless displayed properly and attractively. Once a year, I stroll around my condo looking for items I can list for sale. I have dug up some real dogs. If I put enough lipstick on them, I can usually get someone to bite. It's the ones that don't need lipstick that give me the most trouble as I mistakenly believe they will sell themselves given their already pristine condition. But what I've learned is they need lipstick, too. If not properly presented, it makes no difference what condition the item is in. The market simply won't give it a chance.

A similar phenomenon unfolds within corporations. And here's why. As stated previously, in order for a corporation to stay alive indefinitely, it must continually be hiring and promoting employees to backfill those who retire and/or are promoted up through the ranks. To be successful at this, especially when selecting those to promote, corporations must look towards their organization's dominance hierarchy and react accordingly. But given the incredibly large stakes at hand, the final say for these decisions is almost never left with the front-line managers. Rather, they are delegated to an executive further up the chain. The issue arises when that executive is asked to make decisions on people they've had minimal interaction with and thus know nothing about. This creates a unique situation where the corporation is forced to find creative ways to showcase these employee's abilities to those executives through carefully crafted assignments. In the corporate world, this is referred to as "gaining exposure".

Attaining this exposure is no simple task, even if you've worked your way to the top of the hierarchy. In a perfect world, that would make you a shoe-in for such assign-ments. But what you must realize is that hierarchical rankings aside, corporations don't always get things right. You must never assume that just because you worked yourself to the top of the dominance hierarchy that you'll automatically be the one the corporation chooses to place in front of the final decision-makers. To be selected, every advantage must be exploited to maximize your odds. Your clothing is one such advantage.

Now, ask yourself this. If you were the decision-maker responsible for assigning these high-visibility assignments, and assuming all else was equal between two possible candidates, who would you assign them to? Thinking back to the eBay example, would it be the one who went the extra mile to ensure they presented themselves in a proper and respectable manner, or the one who didn't?

In corporations, what you're capable of bringing to the table means nothing if you're never given the chance to bring it. You could be Albert Einstein, for all that matters. This is what having the right clothing can do for you. You must present yourself in a manner that will inspire others to take a chance on you. If you don't, it will make no difference how smart or capable you may be.

Helping to secure high exposure projects during your early years isn't the only thing proper clothing can do for you. There are many other advantages beyond this. Example. Fast forward a few years into your career. Your company has a client coming in town that could possibly produce the largest deal of the year. But it coincides with all the executives going to Hawaii for their annual lead-ership conference. This leaves them scrambling to find an employee with the skills and experience to make the pitch and secure the deal. After a few days of deliberation, they've narrowed the field down to two possible candi-dates. And guess what? You made the final two. But they are at a standstill. Both you and your fellow employee who made the cut have the exact same level of experience, talent, and raw ability. It's now down to one last determining factor. *Who looks the most presentable.*

I know this sounds basic, but I'm constantly dumbstruck at the number of people who get this wrong and have their careers suffer for it. These one-off opportunities are rare and capitalizing on them can have significant impacts on the long-term trajectory of your career. You must do whatever it takes to secure them. That said, your clothing should be considered an investment, not an expense. A stock, for instance. When purchased, the expectation is your investment will generate a return at some point in the future. Clothing should be thought of no differently. If done properly, doors will be opened and opportunities will be given that you otherwise wouldn't have been exposed to, boosting your future earnings potential should you do well with them.

Let's now talk cost. The initial outlay for a decent wardrobe can be frightening, especially with an exclusive clothier like Brooks Brothers. For a mere five to ten thousand dollars, they will certainly set you on the right path. But at this stage in your career, for more than just the obvious reason of expense, this is not where you belong. There is quality clothing to be had at fractional prices that will generate as good if not better results than the high-end outlets. What matters is how its worn, not the cost. There are many in this world who spend a fortune only to look like an exotic bird as soon as they step into the office.

It's worth mentioning that even for astute shoppers, buying clothes can be a pain. But as the saying goes, no pain no gain. You must put in the effort. If not, you will be looked over time and time again when the aforementioned opportunities present themselves as corporations will rarely, if ever, put a slob in front of clients.

Here is my advice. Start small and start early. Building a wardrobe takes time, especially on a budget. The retail industry thrives on people who buy on impulse. You must beat them at their own game (i.e. waiting until the fourth week of January for the "real" after-Christmas sale). I personally don't buy anything unless it's fifty to eighty percent off. But this requires patience and the ability to purchase well ahead of your need time. If you procrastinate until the last second you will overspend as it allows stores to dictate what price you pay for their goods. You should only purchase items when stores need you more than you need them. This happens at the end of each season when they are clearing unsold inventory to make way for the next season. For example, March and April are excellent times to purchase fall/winter items as stores move inventory to make way for summer. This is not when you *want* to buy these items given it's almost summer, but that's exactly why they are so much cheaper this time of year. Demand drops which forces corresponding price drops. It's basic economics. High supply plus low demand equals great pricing.

We've now covered several avenues in which proper clothing can help open doors within major corporations. First, it provides an edge over your peers when securing high visibility assignments that provide exposure to the decision-makers. Second, it assists with attaining roles in critical business interactions that lead to bigger opportunities should you be successful in them. The last avenue we will cover is this. By properly dressing, not only are you making yourself look respectful and presentable, but you're also sending an important signal to the corporation that you know how to *properly prepare*.

In the business world, proper preparation is what separates the good employees from the great employees. What most fail to realize is clothing choices are an easy way to demonstrate these skills, especially for new employees who haven't yet been with the company long enough to prove them through other means. But why is it important to demonstrate your ability to prepare right off the bat? Because the corporation will use this as one of many indicators as to how you will behave in a business setting. These indicators will then be used to distribute those ever-so critical starting assignments.

You may believe this is splitting hairs, which it is. But you must remember that in a major corporation, you're on a razors edge at all times and what may seem like a small thing today could grow into something exponentially larger five years down the road. These initial assignments are a prime example of this. They will never be of equal weighting—some will undoubtedly be more complex and rewarding than others. But if received, larger doors will be opened if successful with them. This is done by design. The best assignments are allocated to those deemed to have the most potential. Corporations want to get these individuals up and running as fast as possible. Will the employees third in line eventually get their chance at one of these assignments? Probably. But by the time their name is called, the person who received theirs on day one will have already scored numerous touchdowns given their head start. Be prepared and get it right from the outset. Trust me, in ten years you will thank yourself for it.

Principle #2:
*Clothing should deter attention, not attract it.*

As a young man, I was highly materialistic and overly obsessed with image and status. As embarrassing as it is to talk about, it taught me an important lesson. You earn respect from others by living within yourself and your means and not vice versa. Why is that? Because when you succeed at something, life will reward you through one of many ways—financially, socially, emotionally, or spiritually. The problem arises when people skip the work

part and go straight for the reward without properly earning it, just as I was doing. This leaves two distinct groups
representing the same level of societal status—those who
earned it and those who didn't. An inefficiency within
the ranks is then created leading to inordinate amounts
of friction between the groups. If left unresolved, this
friction will boil over, leading to catastrophic consequences—particularly for those representing a status of
which they did not earn. And here's why.

Picture a sixty-year-old man who saved his entire
life to finally buy his dream car. While out driving, he
comes across a sixteen-year-old kid with the same car.
He immediately thinks to himself, "What a spoiled brat!"
Step back and think about what just happened. In a split
second, this man's opinion of that kid was instantly transformed because he was driving something he obviously
didn't *earn*. And, it had nothing to do with the kid himself or what his actual abilities in life may have been.

Now, take that same kid but instead put him in a twen-
ty-year-old beater. What does the old man think of him
then? He'd instantly give him more respect as he is driving something within his "range" (i.e. the level of societal
status earned in life). He is living within his means and
in the eyes of the world that's all that matters. Respect
earned.

What does this have to do with clothing inside a corporation? Everything. In corporations, you, too will run
into this issue. But it's your clothing, not your car, that
that will be scrutinized. In corporations, as in society,
there are certain levels of "status" you can earn. These
levels correlate to your ranking within the organization.
But no longer are they represented by the type of car you
drive. Rather, by type and quality of the clothing you
wear. It's therefore *critical* that you don't overdress your
specific range as doing so can lead to friction between you
and the people who actually earned that range. But who

cares if it causes friction? I mean, what's the big deal? The big deal is you're no longer pissing off a random person on the street. Rather, it's your superiors within the corporation who have complete control over of your career advancement, or lack thereof.

Dressing within your range prevents you from attracting the wrong types of attention. This keeps others focused on what's really important—your work products. To implement this strategy, start by identifying the specific ranges within your company. The following is likely a fair representation of such ranges. Top executives favor suits and footwear that cost in the thousands. Directors and first-level VPs wear specialty clothier store fashions. Mid-level management dress in pricey business professional styles. And mid to lower level non-managerial employees are often in department store clothing.

Now, within these ranges, there's certainly some flexibility. Not much, but some. So, while you want to stay within your range, the trick is to dress as close to the next range without actually crossing the line. Doing so will not only keep you in the best graces of your management, but will also make you the best-dressed employee within the organization, regardless of which range you reside in.

But what about those who blow their entire paycheck on the fanciest, most extravagant clothes possible? Shouldn't they be seen as the best-dressed employees? Not exactly. Most overdo it and end up dressing themselves way out of their current range. However, when someone is able to maintain their range but push it to the absolute limit without crossing into the next level, it presents the same effect as does a high-quality and minimally applied fragrance. When you first walk by the person wearing it, you don't even notice. But five or ten seconds later you think to yourself, "Wow, that person smelled good!" Your clothing should be no different. You don't want to smack people in the face with it. It should go unnoticed at first. It's not until a few looks later that it hits them and they can't help but ask what you're wearing or where you shop.

To summarize, proper clothing is that which makes you feel the most comfortable. But not physically comfortable. Rather, *psychologically* comfortable. If you stay dressed within your range, you'll be at peace, allowing your mind to remain focused on what's important—accomplishing your assignments. If you show up dressed out of your range, you'll constantly be burdened with people looking at you funny and giving you the cold shoulder—exactly the kind of attention to avoid as a new employee.

As you progress in your career, you will certainly move into the higher ranges. But don't put the cart in front of the horse. Wait for your time—you will earn more respect by doing so. But this doesn't mean you shouldn't be preparing for the next range ahead of time should you see yourself moving into it. Remember, building a wardrobe takes time, especially on a budget. You don't want to be stuck wearing the same clothing from your prior range because you didn't properly prepare ahead of time.

I'll finish with one last advantage proper clothing can provide you in a major corporation. Throughout this book, I stated that for corporations to survive indefinitely, they must continually attract and hire the best available talent to backfill those who vacate their positions for various reasons. Filling these vacancies is a never-ending process that takes an incredible amount of time and resources. But it's a necessary evil as corporations must remained staffed at levels necessary to satisfy the demand for its products. That said, there are several challenges that corporations face when recruiting these top-level individuals. First, the candidate pool contains a finite number of individuals. And second, every other corporation in their industry is also trying to recruit from that very same pool. Given these constraints, corporations must use every trick in the book to land these people at their company. But what most corporate employees fail to realize is just how lucrative this recruitment process can be for them. Should you be one who can easily attract and land those top recruits, the corporation will put you on a pedestal as you are saving the company untold amounts of money by lowering their recruiting cost. That money can then be redirected to other projects. But how do you become one of these people? It's simple. You transform yourself into the most presentable, classiest-looking employee the company has to offer. Think about it. What would a potential new-hire think if their first encounter with the company was with someone who looked like a frumpy, wrinkled mess? Odds are they would instantly be turned off. It's no different than that uncomfortable feeling you get when walking into an outdated, musty grocery store. Even though their groceries may not be any different than those at the newer store down the street, given its appearance, all excitement is lost as soon as you step foot through its doors. The same thing can happen to a potential new hire. If the first thing they see is a slob with wrinkled pants and stains on their shirt, they'll get the musty old grocery store effect and will be turned off to your company. Corporations can't afford this to happen. Therefore, they will put the most presentable employees on the front lines as they are viewed by recruits as a direct reflection of the company itself.

# VIII: CORPORATE LANDMINES - WATCH WHERE YOU STEP

POP QUIZ. WHAT DO PAINTERS and corporate employees have in common? Answer—they are both one stroke away from catastrophic failure. Think about it. What happens when an artist accidently puts black paint where they were supposed to put white paint? Their painting is destroyed. Off to the trash it goes. They made a mistake of such severity that it cannot be fixed regardless how hard they try. But don't get me wrong. Many mistakes can be corrected by adjusting the design or by painting over it. However, this chapter isn't about those mistakes. It's about the ones that have the power to not only ruin a painting, but a career.

As a corporate employee, the truth is that you, too, will constantly be one "stroke" away from completely derailing your career. And, it makes no difference whether you're a new employee or the CEO. But this chapter isn't about the obvious—lying, stealing, cheating, or anything criminal. These are the no-brainers. Rather, it's about those buried far below the surface, never to be seen in a corporate rule book. These, my friends, are the *landmines*.

Throughout my career, I've identified what I believe are the ten most dangerous landmines that exist within corporate America. I've seen many individuals step on these—most never saw it coming, myself included. They are in no particular order and are all of equal importance.

## Landmine #1:
### Complacency Kills

For anyone that is familiar with my hometown of Houston, you're well aware of just how hot the summers can get. The problem is that unlike other areas which can reach over one hundred degrees during those mid to late summer months, Houston can also be extremely humid. And, when mixed with the intense heat, you're left with a smoldering stew that leaves you drenched as soon as you step outside.

While in college, I spent the summers working for a friend's air conditioning business. It was the most difficult work I have ever experienced—everything from spending all day installing new ductwork to changing out complete systems in attics where temperatures soared to over one hundred forty degrees. Anytime I'm having a tough day in my corporate job, I think back to those job sites and quickly realize my hardest days in the office are a cakewalk compared to my best days working in the A/C business.

There was one day in particular I will never forget. We were doing a full change-out for a customer that required us to be in the attic for the majority of the day. When you work in the A/C business, the first thing you're taught is to avoid the "soft spots" while walking through attics. If you step on one, you will fall through the ceiling and onto the floor below. Countless technicians have succumbed to this mistake, many who survived the fall. But there are others who didn't get so lucky and wound up seriously injured. A common saying the A/C business states, "There are those who have stepped through a ceiling and those who haven't stepped through a ceiling, *yet*". I was a part of the latter and was doing everything I could to avoid this costly mistake. And then it happened. While carrying out the old unit, I joined the club. I slipped on a piece of wood, sending my left foot crashing through the celling below me. Miraculously, as I was falling, my shoulder caught the attic wall, allowing me to regain my balance back onto the support beam.

As traumatizing as that experience was, it taught me a valuable lesson. It doesn't matter how well you performed in the past. If you don't put the same level of focus on your work today as you did then, you can fall through the attic just as I nearly did. But how does this relate to corporations? Like attics, corporations don't care what you did yesterday. The only thing that matters is what can you do *today*. Just because you are a master technician who's flawlessly changed hundreds of units in the past does not mean the attic floor will provide you any more leniency than the next person. The result will be the same.

But what happens if you screw up and actually fall through? Will the corporation leave you there? Or will they help you up so you can continue working? It depends. As stated numerous times, corporations do what makes them the most money. They are the definition of greed, driven and owned by greedy stockholders who care about one thing—increasing the stock price. Therefore, any stumbles will be written off as anomalies so long as they believe it not to be your new baseline level of performance. But if your performance reaches the point where the corporation believes you've truly lost it, they will no longer help you up off the floor. Rather, they'll leave you there shattered and broken while they go in search for their next rock star.

Let's cover one last example regarding the danger of complacency in corporations. My entire life, I've had problems getting a good haircut. I don't know what it is, but I've been through more barbers than anybody you've ever known. While writing this book, it finally hit me as to why it keeps happening. It's the same reason that experienced A/C technicians fall through attic ceilings—complacency. You see, my bad haircuts don't start the first time I see a new barber. They are quite good the initial visit, and usually a couple more after that. But I noticed once the barber realizes I'm going to be a full-time client, their performance declines. And, these aren't run of the mill barbershops. They are high-end barbers who hold themselves to exacting standards. Even with that, they become complacent once I'm "locked in", forcing me to move to another barber. Because of this, I implemented a new strategy. It's called three and go. Three haircuts and I move to the next one. That way I'm guaranteed a fresh, "new client" haircut every time I sit in the chair.

The point of this landmine is you must continue to perform. And, it doesn't matter if you're a seasoned professional or a brand-new employee. You must perform at the minimum on same level which you did in the past to preserve your standing within the corporation. Do this and you'll be just fine. Become complacent and watch your career die a slow and painful death.

### Landmine #2:
### Being "Too Smart"

Make no mistake, being smart is great. You can solve problems easier, read other people's minds, and are more likely not to be scammed. But to be honest, intelligence has its limits. Particularly when working for a major corporation. And here's why.

Back in chapter three, I discussed how corporations operate similar to ski lifts when satisfying their never-ending need for human capital. I also discussed how they won't allow an employee up to the more difficult slopes until they gather the necessary skills and experience required to ski down them. But what if a new hire already possesses these skills (i.e., a natural born "skier")?

Will the corporation immediately open the gates and promote them without hesitation? Absolutely not. Just because they can handle the speed of a double black diamond slope doesn't mean they can also handle the severe right-hand turn just over the crest that they didn't see coming. This is precisely why corporations will first and foremost require their employees to be of a certain level of experience prior to sending them up the chain, regardless of how talented they may be. After all, it's this experience which enables them to foresee those tricky turns long before anyone else, allowing them to navigate them safely where other, less experienced employees would most certainly crash.

It all comes down to risk management. There's too much on the line in terms of potential financial impacts for corporations to promote unproven and inexperienced individuals to levels where catastrophic damage could occur should they crash and burn. "But, but... they were the next Einstein!" Too bad – nobody, especially the shareholders, will care. All they care about is their stock price, not the dreams of some twenty-three-year old kid. Good as they may be, the experience must be there. It's a non-negotiable. Period.

That said, if you're a new employee trying to fly up ladder, how smart do you think it would be to blow off experience-building opportunities? Not very. But you'd be amazed at how many times I've seen it happen because someone thought an assignment was "below them".

The truth is that some young employees, particularly the super-bright ones, will sometimes feel the level of assignments given to them aren't intellectually challenging enough to waste their time on. Said another way, they believe they are *too smart* for such work. But rejecting such assignments is one of the most dangerous and detrimental moves any single person can make inside a major corporation. Why? Because they are much more than just meaningless assignments. Rather, they are experience-building opportunities the corporation is providing to qualify yourself for more complex assignments down the road.

Let me put this in a different context. As I was driving to work the other day, I began staring at the plastic cover that goes over my cigarette lighter. I started thinking to myself, out of all the components that make this vehicle run, the manufacturer actually had to dedicate one of its engineers to design this tiny piece before they could begin fabrication of the vehicle. And, I'm not talking about anything super complicated. A fifth grader could have done it. But had it not been completed my vehicle wouldn't have made it through final production.

My point is this. Just because the cigarette lighter cover isn't nearly as complex as some of the other components, such as the engine or the twelve-way duel reclining seats, it's still required for final product delivery. Did it take the same amount of brain power to design? Probably not. Did the engineer who completed the design receive praise within the corporation for doing it? Nope. Has the vice president of engineering at some point in their career spent time designing these little pieces? You bet your ass they have. Not only have they had jobs in the "cigarette lighter cover" department, but in every other department within the engineering organization. Here's why.

Let's hypothetically say that a major car manufacturer allowed someone to run their engineering organization who was a brilliant individual but didn't have the necessary experience to know if certain design teams were doing what they were supposed to be doing. What do you think would happen? They would put lives at risk. If they are unable to tell the difference between a good design and a bad one and sign off on it anyways, they're not only putting the company at risk for delivering a faulty product, but also the lives of their customers who drive the vehicles. It's therefore critical for corporations to ensure those who are promoted up the chain have a broad range of experiences within the company as it allows them to recognize whether the work being produced by the employees beneath them is done at levels sufficient enough to meet company standards.

What this landmine boils down to is liability. It makes no difference how smart or talented you may be—the corporation isn't going to promote you without the required experience. Doing so may not result in such extreme consequences as described above, but it could certainly impact the bottom line. The problem arises when you have incredibly smart, driven, and talented young individuals who enter the corporation without understanding this piece of the corporate equation and become frustrated when assigned tasks below their intelligence level without first realizing the corporation is just checking their boxes before promoting them up the chain. This leads them to respond with anger and resentment towards the company, neither which are beneficial to their careers.

Let me be clear—I'm not saying it isn't ok to be smart. It's absolutely ok. You just can't keep your foot on the throttle one hundred percent of the time. Corporations don't work that way. Will you be given opportunities for straightaways where you can max yourself out? Absolutely. But so, too, will there be times where the road becomes curvy and you must ride the brake for a while. Having the wherewithal to identify and adjust your intelligence to these varying situations is what it means to be *truly smart* in a major corporation.

<u>*Landmine #3:*</u>
*Refusing the "Corporate Kool-Aid"*

Make no mistake. I love cherry Kool-Aid. But in the spirit of keeping my weight down, I decided it was no longer an option as its sugar content didn't bode well with my weight loss goals. It was a very sad moment. This led to one of my greatest discoveries in life; sugar free cherry Kool-Aid. It was an immediate game-changer. I could now quench my sensational appetite without all the health consequences. I eventually moved to other flavors with some success, but none of which satisfied me like my beloved cherry.

In corporations, you, too, will be drinking a lot of Kool-Aid. But unlike my addiction where I could switch flavors whenever I wanted, you will not have that option. If the flavor of the day is tropical and you're a grape person, too bad. You must make the switch. Your personal preferences are now meaningless and any hesitation will put you at risk for incredible harm. And when I say harm, I don't mean harm to your body. Rather, I mean harm to your career.

It was around the third year of my career when I first experienced the Kool-Aid phenomenon. I'm not exactly sure where he got it, but the president of our division was stuck on the idea that we needed to go through a magnificent and grandiose culture change in order create an environment where the newer generation would feel more "comfortable". In today's marketplace, I completely agree that culture plays a critical part in determining a corporation's success as it defines how employees interact with each other. These interactions drive productivity levels throughout the organization and cannot be constrained in any way, shape, or form. This is precisely why corporations are placing so much emphasis on optimizing their culture as they have finally realized the incredibly strong connection between it and the bottom line. That said, I completely understand why my company prioritized it and thought it to be a really cool thing for them to be doing.

But as rosy as that may sound, the actual implementation process is far from it. Normal protocol is for the executive driving the change to shove so much culture bullshit down your throat that you can barely breathe. Culture books, culture value pyramids, algebraic culture equations, culture town halls...you name it. The problem arises not with the first one you go through as the spiel can sound fairly interesting. It's the next one, and the next one after that, and the next one after that one, and so on. You see, in major corporations, these "culture changes" are as closely tied to the executive trying to implement them as is the two hundred–dollar tie that is wrapped around their neck. And when that executive leaves or retires, guess what? Their "tie" goes with them. So, that's it, right? Time to get back to normal? Not quite.

Fortunately for you, the next executive in line is going to have yet another fabulous idea for how to improve the culture across the corporation. But why another one? Because executives are suckers for overpaid consultants selling click-bait programs that promise to deliver the world should they buy their service. Therefore, anytime a new executive comes into the organization the cycle will repeat itself and you will once again be force-fed the exact same culture bullshit. It will just be a different flavor than what the last one fed you as every executive must distinguish themselves in their own unique way.

Here's where things can become extremely dangerous for you and your career. Let's say you really liked the *last* executive's flavor. But after one week of the new person's flavor, you decide it's not for you and refuse to drink it. Guess what happens next? You're sent to what's called corporate timeout where there's no such thing as raises, promotions, or opportunities. And, you'll stay there for as long as you refuse to drink up. You are now considered a renegade by the new executive, a renegade who could potentially impact their bonus. This, my friends, is what it means to refuse the corporate Kool-Aid.

A culture change is just one example of many where you must constantly adapt to the countless flavors of bullshit the corporation will constantly be feeding you. But your method for success for each and every one of them will remain the same: *Suck it up, buttercup.* If you want succeed in a corporation, it doesn't matter what your preferences are. You are now abiding by someone else's rules—they could not give a damn if you are a cherry lover. If the flavor of the day is tropical sour grape, guess what your new favorite flavor is? So hold your nose, close your eyes, scratch your thigh, whatever. Just drink the shit. Eventually it will blow over once the executive realizes the real work isn't getting done because everybody is too busy powdering their assess all day dealing with the massive amounts of non-work-related garbage that comes with these initiatives.

One last thing before we move on. Be very careful never to become a "culture warrior" who parades around the office attempting to force-feed fellow coworkers the latest round of culture happy nonsense. Only a small percentage of employees actually buy into these changes and pushing it upon a non-believer could potentially ruin your relationship with that person. For all you know they could be as much against it as you are for it. This all ties back to the earlier discussion about how making your way through a corporation is like driving on a busy highway. To avoid crashing, you must always be adapting to others around you. This is a textbook example of that. If your coworker is in the slow lane doing fifty-five and you come up beside them trying to shove one hundred miles per hour worth of culture bullshit down their throat, it could potentially cause a major accident between you and that person. A failed relationship would result along with complete elimination of your access to their chapter in the corporate textbook—a mistake that must be avoided at all cost.

### Landmine #4:
### Run Your Own Race

Running – what a horrible idea. After spending many years pounding pavement in everything from 10Ks to twenty mile-a-week run schedules, I reserve the right to say that anyone who claims to enjoy running is a brain-washed liar. There is absolutely nothing "fun" about running. Just ask my achy feet and wobbly knees! I will say that regardless of how miserable my running years were, it taught me many valuable lessons, some which carried over to life inside a major corporation.

Ask any runner their strategy for running their best times and I guarantee most will give the same answer— to run within themselves. What does this mean? It means that in order to post a good time, they need to run at a pace their body can handle and sustain throughout the entire race. Otherwise, they put themselves at risk for early burnout. Can they post a faster time by sprinting the first three-quarters and walking the last one-fourth? It's possible. But a more consistent and reliable approach is to run a more conservative pace throughout. You especially see this in cycling. I don't think I've ever watched a single race on TV and there not been a guy who comes out sprinting only to be gassed by the final stretch and be caught by their competitors who better paced themselves. Why does this happen? My guess is lack of training—they become intimidated by their competition and overexert themselves to keep up. The more experienced cyclists resist this temptation and conserve energy so they can perform at their peak throughout the entire race.

This phenomenon can just as easily take hold inside a corporation as it can with runners trying to post their best time. Bad "run times" are the equivalent of mistakes and embarrassing rework and your competition is now fellow coworkers instead of other runners. But one thing remains constant—all that matters is results. Will there be others who are smarter, harder working, and better polished than you? Of course, that's just a fact of life. However, the key to producing your best "times" inside a corporation is to maximize your individual potential, not your stress by trying to keep up with somebody who may be on a different path than you. Remember, not everybody can be the CEO.

Maximizing your individual potential inside a major corporation boils down to two things. First, working within yourself and your own personal constraints to complete your assignments with the absolute highest level of quality and workmanship. And second, producing them within the overall timeline which the corporation has given you. In a perfect world, the corporation will adjust these deadlines to correlate with the time you personally need to get the job done. But in reality, you will oftentimes be given aggressive deadlines that don't fall within your "race pace", leaving you one of two options. First, to continue at your regular pace working additional hours via late nights and weekends to get the assignment done. That's obviously not the most appealing choice, causing most to fall into the deadly trap of option two—working the same number of hours and *increasing* their pace. As with running, falling for this trap can be extremely, and I mean *extremely*, detrimental to your career. Why? Because you will start making mistakes, lots of them. And when you make mistakes, several things happen. First, you end up doing rework to fix the errors, making the overall time to complete the project far greater than it would have been had you just worked at your normal pace to begin with. And second, your reputation will reflect as one who does substandard work, forcing the corporation to give you fewer and fewer assignments. And the fewer assignments you receive, the less value you're adding to the bottom line. This sends your reputation into a vicious downward descent, one that is almost impossible to pull yourself out of. It's like an airplane that loses control and goes into a "death spiral", rapidly moving towards the earth's surface before crashing and plunging into flames.

But won't putting the quality of your work over the corporation's deadlines cause you to get dinged? Probably. But not all dings are equal. The dings you receive from missing deadlines are microscopic in comparison to those created from errors being uncovered in your work. And in my experience, it's a ten to one ratio. It takes at least ten from missed deadlines to equal one from a mistake. The corporation however isn't going to tell you this. They want you to think that missing a deadline is the absolute worst thing you could do as an employee. But this is far from the truth. Remember, the corporation has one interest only. Itself. Not you, not your coworker, not your boss. Itself. And as stated earlier in the book, you must realize that as much as you want to help the corporation succeed, it shouldn't be your number one priority. Your number one priority is figuring out how to succeed *within it*. Run your own race and produce quality work time after time and you will do just that. Succumb to the pressure of deadlines at the expense of your workmanship and watch your career fall apart—one deadline at a time.

### Landmine #5:
### The Art of the Mistake

While there is no leniency for mistakes resulting from poor workmanship as described above, the truth is not all mistakes are bad. There is another type of mistake that you can and will make inside a corporation. And, these mistakes can be used to your advantage. So, what are they? They are ones you make because you have no earthly idea what you're doing as a new employee. They are also the kind that if played correctly can pay big dividends, sending you to levels you may never have thought possible. But you must be incredibly careful. These mistakes can just as easily destroy your career as they can promote it. Once made, you have a split second to decide how you're going to respond. Respond correctly, they can and will become one of your greatest assets. Let me explain.

I have always been fascinated that humans once lived on this planet with nothing more than the skin on their bodies and hair on their heads. They had no cars, no microwaves, no weapons, no comfy beds, and certainly no smartphones. If they needed something, they had to make it using whatever resources were available at the time. And unlike today, back then it was a very simple equation. Create what you need to survive or die. There were no two ways around it.

Fast forward to today. Look around you. What do you see? Unless you're a nomad living in the desert somewhere, you probably see things. Lots and lots of things. You could see a car, a desk, a chair, a wall, a computer, or a smartphone. Regardless of the object, none of them were created out of thin air. At some point there was a human who needed these items—a need they turned into reality by following their passion and drive to do so. What blows my mind is how we take these items for granted. Electricity, gas-heated homes, airplanes, the internet...the list could go forever. Unfortunately, as the generations come and go, so too goes the realization of what it took to pull these inventions off. All we care about is how to get one, not how it got here.

While each of these inventions started as an idea, they never could have materialized had it not have been for some brave soul having the courage to roll up their sleeves and figure a way to make it happen. But how did they know where to start? Was there an instruction pamphlet showing them what to do? Absolutely not. They simply followed their passion and allowed the mistakes they made along the way to guide them across the finish line. Let me say that again. *They allowed the mistakes they made along the way to guide them across the finish line.*

The smartest people in the world all realize that mistakes can be one of their most powerful assets if treated properly. They understand they are life's way of giving us "free advice" in order to shape our ideas into the fabulous creations they were meant to be. It's no different than an artist who uses their hands to slowly mold a block of clay into a beautiful piece of art. No matter how good they are, there will always be bumps and imperfections to work through prior to its completion.

This is why you should never run from your mistakes as a new employee. Why? Because your manager will be *expecting* you to make mistakes—lots of them. It's part of the development process. And, they'll know when and where you're going to make them. How? Because many others have occupied your job prior to your arrival (and since moved on), allowing your company to pinpoint exactly where the stumbling blocks are. This is also where you can get yourself into *serious* trouble. The reason is that while yes, mistakes can be an incredibly useful tool at your disposal if you have the willingness to learn from them, they are also what management uses to *test your trustworthiness.* If you cover them up when your manager already knows you're going to make them, how do you think that's going to work out for you? Hint—not very well.

How you react to mistakes is one of many ways the corporation will test your trustworthiness. Another commonly used method is to ask you questions they already know the answer to. These are carefully designed so that your honesty, or lack thereof, can be gauged by your response. I have seen this trickery catch many in outright lies. But had they familiarized themselves with one simple phrase, it could have been avoided. *"I don't know"*. Using this phrase requires incredible humility, but once mastered, it can be one of the most powerful tools you have at your disposal as a new employee. Its use will not only protect the most sacred asset you have within a corporation—your trust, but will also earn you respect as it provides a golden opportunity to go research and provide a timely follow up, both which are critical skills that corporations love to see in their employees.

To summarize, the phrase, "Once a liar, always a liar", runs just as true in corporations as it does in life. If you lose the trust of your management, you're as good as dead. There is nothing worse that can happen to you inside a corporation. It's the bottom the barrel. Start applying to other companies because it won't be long before they conveniently lay you off during the next "re-org". I have witnessed many coworkers lie about their mistakes, all whose careers were immediately put in neutral once management lost trust in them. Most were forced to leave in search of a fresh start. For those who didn't, well, they are still sitting in neutral, many years down the road. Don't make the same mistake they did.

### *Landmine #6:*
### *Stability Issues? Forget About It.*

My typical day involves sitting at a computer and staring at numbers for nine hours straight. Given the health issues this could produce, I take several walks throughout the day to get my blood flowing. It's during these walks where I recharge, deliberate problems, be inspired, and mentally prepare myself for both my immediate and long-term future. It's also when I go into deep thoughts about not only the contents of this book, but where it might take me one day. The ultimate goal is speaking with college students across the country about the realities of working for a major corporation. My biggest fear however is being asked how high I made it within my corporation while still working. I worry I could lose all credibility if my response is anything short of CEO, hindering my ability to successfully communicate my message. After all, you would think a guy who wrote a book on how to be successful in a major corporation should have at least been, well, successful in a major corporation.

The truth is this. My career is doing just fine. But I'm certainly not the CEO and probably never will be. Would I like to be? Maybe—I honestly believe I have what it takes to lead at that high of a level. But regardless of my abilities, I've had too many hang-ups along the way which derailed my career from all that could have been. Or said another way, I stepped on too many damn landmines! After all, I didn't dream these up in my sleep.

My biggest derailment came during the sixth year of my career. I was twenty-eight and had secured a reputation as one of the most talented young employees the company had. It was a peculiar position for me to be in, one that I was unfamiliar with as I was a very late bloomer, not realizing my full potential until my mid-twenties. But when I did, things really took off. It was also when all hell broke loose in my life. I entered a dark period triggered by a series of personal missteps which exposed many issues buried deep within me. During the worst, I was in pure survival mode, living day to day with only one goal in mind—make it to the next day.

As traumatic as this period was, I survived and learned many valuable lessons along the way. One in particular will never leave me. If you want to be fast-tracked in a major corporation, have your personal life in order. If you don't, the corporation will pull the emergency brake on your career faster than you can blink. Will they show compassion, patience, and sympathy towards you and your struggles? It's possible. Mine thankfully did.

If you're fortunate enough to be put on the "fast-track" in a major corporation, you must remember one thing. The corporation is preparing you for a position of power which comes with far greater levels of responsibility than anything you could ever imagine. Not only will you be responsible for your own output in one of these jobs, but also the output of each employee within the organization which you reside over. When my company pulled the emergency brake on me, I took it very personally. But knowing what I know now, it all makes sense. They had no choice. They had to do what was best for the bottom line and placing me in a high-level position would have added too much risk to the business. I was put on the backburner, and rightfully so. Think of it like a ship's captain. What would happen if they were unable to keep a steady hand on the wheel? Worst case is they wreck the ship, killing everyone on board. The same goes for corporations. While employees obviously won't die if the "captain" crashes, they will be left leaderless, creating a potentially toxic situation. Scattering in all different directions, these unguided workers will create utter chaos within the ranks, bringing not only themselves down, but other employees as well.

If your personal life isn't in order, it won't matter how talented or qualified you may be. If there's any risk whatsoever that you could potentially "sink the ship" because you're not stable enough to drive it, you'll be skipped over in favor of the next candidate. So, do what you have to do to get your shit together. If you do run into personal issues, keep them to yourself. Don't feel like you have to tell the corporation. They can and will use it against you whether they tell you or not. And, when I say keep your mouth shut, I seriously mean keep it shut. Telling one person is the same as telling the entire corporation. Remember, people in corporations love to talk, especially about other people's problems. Giving them a nugget on your personal life is like giving a piece of chicken to a hungry crocodile. They will feast on it until there's nothing left. So, do what's required to fix your issues and keep a smile on your face until you get through it. As the saying goes, "fake it till ya make it". And remember, this, too, shall pass.

*Landmine #7:*
*The Corporate Couch Potato*

When I set out to write this book, I had one goal in mind—to teach everything your college didn't regarding what it takes to succeed in a major corporation. By now you should know there's much more to it than taking the knowledge you acquired in your accounting, finance, or marketing courses and applying it to your new job. But this makes me wonder. Just why then do we pay all that money if this knowledge isn't going to do anything for us? Is it because of the contacts we make? That's certainly part of it. But now looking back, I have no doubt the real value in college is that it provides an opportunity to develop a specific skill that will not only propel your success within a corporation, but life as well. What skill is that? It's having the ability to engage your brain whenever, wherever, and however you want. Let me explain.

It was during my junior year in college when I somehow landed myself in a course about sixteenth century rhetoric. And no, it wasn't voluntary. I just procrastinated too long when registering for my electives that semester. I was consequently placed in a class I had absolutely zero interest in—a self-inflicted mistake which I was certain would be the downfall of my academic career. Staring at blank walls sounded better than learning anything about sixteenth century rhetoric. How on Earth would I ever prepare for the exams? I didn't see how I would survive.

When I showed up for the first class, my worst nightmare had come true. I was immediately handed a stack of books and was told to have them all read by the end of the semester. And, these weren't just any books. They were books about, well, sixteenth century rhetoric. But as bad as it may have seemed, it would be one of the most important courses I ever took. No, not because I learned about sixteenth century rhetoric. Rather, because it taught me how to engage my brain even in the face of ultimate resistance. After all, who in their right mind cares about sixteenth century rhetoric? I certainly didn't. Nevertheless, I had a GPA to protect. So, I mustered up every ounce of self-discipline I had and forced myself to begin reading the material. What happened next would be one of the most powerful and influential moments of my entire life.

What I quickly realized is that once I actually sat down and began studying, there was no difference between this course and my other finance courses which I had actual interest in. My mental engagement was just as high. There was, however, a major difference regarding what it took to *begin* studying. It's what I call the brain's "the barrier to entry". Or said another way, the mental wall which must be climbed before one's brain will engage in the material. When it came to my finance courses, this wall was extremely low, making it incredibly easy. Sixteenth century rhetoric however was a different animal. Anytime I would come remotely close to the subject my brain would go bananas and run the other way as fast as it could. But once I conquered the wall of resistance, my brain would immediately latch-on to the material. I could have been studying the history of gymnastics for all that mattered—my brain simply didn't care.

Our brains are designed to work and solve problems. The issue arises when we have preconceived biases regarding the type of material we should and shouldn't be exposing it to. Think of it as your brain's barrier to entry. Exposing it to material which conflicts with these biases creates a wall of mental resistance that must be broken before it will turn itself on. But once breached, your brain will enter into an almost subconscious state where it will absorb anything and everything you put in front of it. This is what I call your brain's sweet spot. When entered, there's nothing in the world that matters besides the task in front of you. The time of day, the attractive person next to you, the tornado outside—all now irrelevant.

In corporations, your ability to access this sweet spot will be the single most important skill to have as a new employee. And just like college, your company will test your ability to access it as soon as you walk in the door. If you can't control your brain to make it receptive to *all* assignments and not just ones you're comfortable with, you'll find yourself struggling to stay afloat. Why? Because as stated previously, corporations must expose their high-potential employees to numerous areas of the business for liability reasons. If you happen to be one of these individuals, the only way to survive is by smashing through any and all mental resistance that comes your way. Otherwise you will remain stuck on the first assignment you're given never to advance on, effectively taking you from a high-performer to a non-performer.

That said, there's another reason corporations thrust their best employees into the blender. It allows them to filter out the weak while exposing those who can handle the additional pressure, leaving only the strongest remaining. These employees put mental biases aside, allowing them to conquer anything from boring admin work to high-visibility projects for the CEO. On the other hand, those who do not have this skill are immediately exposed and filtered out. It's just like panning for gold. The corporation will run as much water over the pan as necessary until all the low-grade dirt is removed and only the gold remains.

Hopefully by now you realize the importance of quickly engaging in your assignments. But what if you aren't able to do so? Well, not only will you be sifted out of the gold pan, but you will also become what I refer to as a *corporate couch potato*. You see, the problem with procrastination is that it's exponential. While delaying one minute may add just one additional foot to your mental wall, delaying two minutes will add three feet. Three minutes will add nine feet, and four minutes will add a whopping eighteen feet. Get the picture? The longer you wait to engage your brain, the harder it becomes to *ever* engage it. It's like going to the gym. The hardest part is pushing through the resistance you hit thirty minutes prior to going. But if successful, it never turns out to be as bad as you had initially thought. However, if you succumb to the resistance and don't go at all, it will be even more difficult to go the next day as the seeds of procrastination will begin feeding upon themselves and start multiplying. Skip one more day after that? Watch out below—you're in for a full-derailment. This is precisely why most New Year's resolutions don't make it past January. People start skipping days and next thing they know their wall of resistance grows so large that it becomes impossible to overcome and they just quit altogether.

To summarize, smashing through walls of mental resistance is a critical skill that must be developed prior to beginning your career. Those "meaningless" classes outside of your core curriculum are a perfect place to do just that. You might think they are a waste of time, and you are correct if only considering the material the class is teaching. But you must realize you are learning how to accomplish tasks and assignments outside your realm of comfort. These courses accomplish this by forcing you to engage your brain even when confronted with the most challenging levels of mental resistance. Without this skill you will be immediately exposed as a corporate couch potato. These employees have short shelf lives and are shown the door fairly quickly. So, fight the resistance with everything you have and engage your brain as soon as possible when confronted with a new task. But remember—there's nobody on this planet who doesn't have a little couch potato in them. It's those who conquer it that rise to the top.

*Landmine #8:*
*"That's Not My Job"*

The other morning while getting ready for work, an interesting debate broke out between the two DJs on my morning talk show. The topic was whether or not people in relationships kept "backup plans" in order to protect themselves from isolation should anything happen to their significant other. After an extensive exchange and numerous call-ins, the results were astoundingly unanimous. While males and females both disliked the thought of being alone someday, it was the *females* who actually planned for it. Hell, some admitted to not only keeping a plan B around, but also a Mr. C and D. Talk about stacking the bench! Regardless of whether or not this is true, when it comes to females, there's certainly one thing that cannot be debated—they love to plan. And, it makes no difference what they are planning, so long as they are planning something, anything. Needless to say, they are always prepared for the worst.

When it comes to life inside a major corporation, you too must be prepared for the worst. Why? Because as with real life, you will have someone sustaining and supporting you as you progress. They will just be supporting your progression through the corporation rather than your progression through life. But should something happen to them, the result will be the same. You'll be stranded with no support system left to uphold you, particularly if you didn't plan for it. So, who exactly is this person? *It's your boss.*

In a perfect world, you could spend your entire career under the same boss and be pulled up the ladder along with them as they themselves advance through the ranks. But as I discussed earlier in the book, every employee has an expiration date. So, while it's certainly possible to piggyback off someone for long periods of time, the party will eventually end when you walk into their office one day and they are nowhere to be found. You'll then be trapped in a deep hole, especially if they were the only person within the corporation whom you've had any significant exposure to. Why? Because this makes them the only person who understands your true value. I refer to it as being trapped in a corporate "value-silo". This occurs when your boss gets hit by a bus, laid off, fired, or the like, making not only their inherent value to the corporation plummet to zero, but yours as well. In other words, you have essentially lost your torch-bearer. And, if you don't have a replacement who can pick it up and continue on with it, you must start from scratch and reprove yourself all over again, a very tough road indeed.

The point I'm making is this. To advance in a corporation, you must be pulled from someone above. The problem arises when that person is the only one in the corporation doing the pulling. If something happens to them, your entire career is jeopardized as the "line" supporting your weight will be snapped, causing you to begin a quick and violent downward decent. In other words, your entire support structure will be lost in the blink of an eye, sending you scrambling to find another person of power to latch onto in hopes of being rescued from your freefall. Sometimes you will be successful, other times not. Either way, it's never a pretty sight. Regardless, I can tell you one thing for certain. You will never end up in this position because you were unlucky or in the wrong place at the wrong time. Every employee's sponsor will eventually move on one day. It happens because you didn't *plan for it.*

Just like some females plan for a Mr. B, C, and D, as a corporate employee, you too must plan for a B, C, and D. The only difference is they will be your backup sponsors, not your backup spouses. But how do you go about doing this? Do you tell the corporation you want exposure to five different bosses all at once? Well, no. But that doesn't mean you can't simultaneously impress multiple other bosses at the same time as your own. The key is finding ways to add value to projects outside of your direct line of responsibilities, something which can easily be done by offering help in times of need.

The most extreme form of this can be seen when a team other than your own is working a critical assignment for the corporation but is lacking the necessary resources to complete it. In these situations, employees from other groups are brought in to assist the struggling group for however long it takes to complete the task. This is referred to as being "loaned out" and is an easy way to gain additional sponsors. Five years down the road the manager you temporarily supported may just be the one that saves your bacon should something happen to your current boss and you need a lifeline to grab ahold of. If you impressed them during your "loaner" period, not only will they throw you that lifeline, but they could promote you into a higher position as a way of paying you back.

Now that we understand the importance of gaining as many sponsors as possible for the reasons stated above, let's discuss a major pitfall many employees fall into that significantly hinders their ability to accomplish this. As previously discussed, to gain additional sponsors you must first expose your abilities to as many managers as possible in ways which allow them to form positive opinions of you. The only way to do this is by working on projects outside your realm of responsibilities. However, many believe their boss will be there forever and see no need to impress anyone other than this person, leading them to refuse any and all work outside of their specific silo. It also leads some to speak the four most poisonous words that can ever be spoken inside a major corporation— *"That's not my job."*

As a new employee, your attitude must be that *everything* is your job. Anything from taking out the trash to working a major project for the CEO—just do it. This will provide you maximum exposure throughout the corporation allowing you to build your sponsor base to the greatest extent possible. After all, what kind of message would you be sending if you actually made a dumpster run? It would show your management that you're hungry to succeed and willing to do whatever it takes to help the corporation achieve its goals, even if that means doing a task way outside your current responsibilities. So, while I'm not necessarily advising you to take out the trash, I am telling you to roll up your sleeves and work on anything and everything you can get your hands on in order to recruit as many sponsors as possible. Oh, and one more thing. Never worry about working on something you really shouldn't be. If that's truly the case, your boss will let you know. That's what they get paid to do.

### *Landmine #9:*
### *Controlling the Uncontrollable*

In golf, you can hit the pin with a perfect shot only to have the ball react wildly and spin backwards off the green and into the water. In poker, you can have pocket aces and lose to pocket kings. In bowling, you can hit the slot just right and end up with a seven-ten split. And in corporations, you could be four times more productive than the person next to you and make a fraction of what they make. Regardless of the situation, the truth is no matter where you look in life, there will inevitably be times when you're faced with less than ideal circumstances that are out of your control. But if handled properly, they can be turned in your favor and used to help propel you through the ranks. Let me explain.

When I first entered the corporate world, I had big dreams. Dreams of working my way up so I could earn a big check and brag to the world about how successful I had become. It was as if I had something to prove. And I did, having not been allowed to realize my full potential sooner in life. But then a beautiful thing happened. For the first time, I found myself surrounded by people who not only wanted me at my best, but *needed* me at my best. I was finally given a platform where I could maximize my abilities to the fullest extent. But this landed me in a very precarious situation as it quickly transformed me into an overly headstrong individual. On one hand, this greatly contributed towards my success in making a name for myself. But there was another, far more dangerous side to my hardheadedness, one that would soon reveal itself in all its tormented glory.

It was around the seventh year of my career when a sweeping change of management occurred within my division. This led to an organizational restructure that I was personally involved in. I however was adamantly opposed to the changes and decided to voice my opinion. Prior to this point, doing so had never been an issue given the clout I had with my previous management. But those individuals were now gone. There was a new sheriff in town and I was walking straight into a buzz saw that would nearly decapitate my entire career, one which I never saw coming. This experience would teach me one of the most important lessons I ever learned about life inside a major corporation. *You cannot control the uncontrol-*

*lable.*

In corporations, as in life, you too will encounter your fair share of uncontrollable circumstances. Some will be in your favor, but many will not. For the favorable ones there is obviously no need to make changes. It's unfavorable ones that will trigger your inner instinct to reverse the circumstance to that of a favorable one. But you must be extremely careful. One wrong move could send you packing. If you falsely identify a circumstance as controllable when it's not, you could land yourself in serious trouble trying to change it. But just how do you know if you're in such a circumstance? *You test the waters.* This is done by firing a few warning shots to see how the circumstance responds prior to diving in. If you feel like it's one you can take on after assessing the feedback you received, then by all means take it on. But if the return fire is fierce and heavy, that's your signal the circumstance more than likely cannot be changed and you should immediately switch to plan B. That being to *deal* with the circumstance.

Where people run into trouble is when they continue pushing on an uncontrollable circumstance even after they have identified it as such. This is because the forces against them are usually much stronger than any force which they are able to exert against it. This is precisely where I made my near fatal mistake regarding the situation I was up against with my company re-org. Deep down I knew I was outgunned. However, I had become so accustomed to getting "my way" under the prior regime that I was oblivious to it being an uncontrollable circumstance and kept blindly marching along like nothing ever changed. This led me straight into HR's office where I spent an entire year untangling the massive mess I had created due to my "behavioral issues". And let me tell you, it got really, really messy. It was like a tangled fishing line with everybody pulling on it from different angles trying to unravel it. The more they pulled, the worse it got. I eventually tucked my tail and admitted defeat, but it was a mistake that nearly tanked my career and one I easily could have avoided.

So, how *should* I have gone about things? Fighting it obviously got me nowhere. As stated earlier, I should have *dealt* with the circumstance rather than fighting my way around the office trying to change it. But how? Take poker for example. How many professional poker players make all their money by only playing premium starting hands? Zero. The majority of the time they play average cards at best as premium hands are only dealt every so often. What do you think would happen if they told the dealer they didn't like their hand and wanted a new one? They would get laughed out of the room. This leaves only one option—to fool their competitors into believing their crap cards are something much, much bigger. And, if they are successful, odds are they will win the hand and take the pot.

Looking back at my situation, there's no doubt that I incorrectly played my hand which caused me to "lose the pot". But I easily could have won it had I just played my cards. I had everyone beat the entire time, I just didn't open my eyes wide enough to see the correct play—to farm my resume out to other companies in search of a better job. With the upgraded job title that I was given as a result of the re-org, I could have attained a forty percent or more raise at another company. So, while the situation may have originally been less than ideal, I had the opportunity to turn it into something much bigger.

My situation is just one of many types of uncontrollable situations that can unfold while working in a major corporation. Another more common example is when employees are given unglamorous work assignments. Specifically, those which fall into the grunt work category. These are the time-consuming, minuscule tasks that receive zero visibility within the corporation but must be done in order for the company to move on. The mistake occurs when an employee tries to control the situation by either refusing to complete the task or by telling their boss they want another assignment, both which are terrible choices. Instead, they should use them to their advantage by focusing not on the work itself, but how they go about completing it. Management loves process improvements—it's money to their ears. If something can be done more efficiently, it will drive down cost and improve the bottom line. If you can prove to the corporation that you're able to make such improvements, you'll immediately be put at the top of your class and be treated like a king for as long as you continue to do so.

I'll finish with this. CEOs aren't CEOs because they only play pocket aces. They are CEOs because they continually win pot after pot regardless of the cards they are dealt. Should you have dreams of becoming one, you, too, must learn to win with any two cards as ninety percent of the hands you'll be given in a major corporation will be less than ideal. But what you must remember is regardless of how bad your hand may be, there will *always* be a way to make it a winner. It just requires an open mind and the boldness to implement non-conforming ideas which may sometimes be at conflict with the preferences of those around you.

### *Landmine #10:*
#### *Emotions are Temporary, Emails are Forever*

Regrets—we all have them. Some bad, some really bad, and some so bad you wish you could eradicate them from your memory forever. But when it comes to regrets, there's unfortunately no magic eraser. Your past is your past and it will be with you forever, like it or not. But avoiding new regrets isn't all that difficult. It just takes

CORPORATIONS 101                       115

having enough self-awareness to first identify and then
extinguish the fundamental emotions which lead to those
regrets prior to engaging in the behaviors which create
them.

When it comes to regrets in my own life, I've certainly had my fair share, most which occurred during my
younger years after drinking too much alcohol. It wasn't
until many years later after realizing the profound effect
it had on my behavior that I gave it up for good. But I
was still fascinated by its powerful ability to drastically
alter one's actions. I began thinking deeply as to why. My
conclusions were simple. First, it messes with your brain's
chemicals, enhancing your emotional state. If you're
happy, you get happier. If you're sad, you get sadder. And
if you're angry, you get angrier. That doesn't sound all
too bad if you leave it at that. Unfortunately, things don't
stop there. As you continue drinking, the second and far
more dangerous side of alcohol kicks in—*acting* on these
emotions. This occurs when the alcohol slowly takes
precedent over your rational thinking in terms of which
controls your behavior. Once this seesaw tips against you,
watch out. It's like cutting a tree—there's no going back
once it starts down. The door will swing wide open for
you to make every terrible decision imaginable, all of
which could have been avoided had you stayed in a regular, sober state of mind.

So, what happens when you sober up the next day and
the seesaw balances back out in favor of rational thinking?
You'll think to yourself, "I can't believe I did that last
night. What was I thinking?" And, this won't happen just
once. Rather, it will happen every time your seesaw gets
thrown out of balance after a night of heavy drinking.
Case in point—drunk texting. Anybody who has ever
had too many cocktails is well aware of how regretful this
can be. The next morning when you sober up, that same
great idea you had not eight hours earlier is now your

worst nightmare as your behavioral seesaw turns back in favor of rational thinking. And in the world of texting, there are unfortunately no takebacks. What's said is said. You then tell yourself you'll never do it again only to go back out the next weekend and repeat the entire process. It's a nasty foe indeed.

The point I'm making is this. Letting your emotions take control of your behavior can be extremely hazardous. And, it can happen just as easily in a corporation as it can after having too many drinks. But instead of alcohol, these heightened emotions will now be driven by a pressure-packed work environment. Regardless of how they are fueled, the risk remains not in the emotion itself, but rather its outlet for expression. In corporations, this occurs through emotionally charged emails to your coworkers. And like drunk texting, the context of these emails can come in various forms, including everything from anger to lust. The issue arises when it's your *emotions*, not your rational thinking, that drives the email in the first place.

When your "behavioral seesaw" gets out of whack in corporation, you immediately feel the need to act on your emotions just as you would after having too many drinks. And just like when you're drunk, you'll seek the quickest and most efficient way possible to do so. This is because a significant amount of anxiety comes with these heightened emotional states, anxiety which cannot be relieved until those emotions are acted upon. In a corporation, there's no faster way to do this than by firing up an email and letting it rip. However, this relief is short-lived. Why? Because once the emotional state passes and your seesaw tips back in favor of rational thinking, just as it does after you sober up from a long night of drinking, you will be left with the exact same results—feelings of regret, despair, and disgust. It's just they are now putting your career at risk instead of a trivial relationship you had with an ex-lover.

Now listen up. If you take one thing away from this book, let it be that emails get more people fired within corporations than everything else *combined*. And, every one of these instances is driven by a charged-up individual whose rational thinking becomes overtaken by an overly aggressive emotional state. This leads them to send emails they normally wouldn't have sent had they been in their regular state of mind. Where people run into problems is falsely believing those emails go no further than the person they were originally directed towards. While that may be the case in some instances, the truth is these emails can and will be forwarded to many other people for a multitude of reasons. And this, my friends, is precisely where the problem arises. While the people directly involved in the specific situation which spurred the email to begin with will be aware of the emotions involved that led to the sender's overly-heightened state, anybody else who wasn't involved and has the email forwarded to them will not. This is where emails become *extremely* dangerous.

Prior to the invention of emails, your emotions and resultant behaviors regarding specific situations were linked only to those directly involved in it. This made it much safer to engage in such behaviors as there was little to no chance that someone who wasn't involved could observe your emotional state without first knowing the context behind what drove it. Emails have completely changed that. Someone's emotional state can now be emailed out to the entire corporation with the click of a mouse. The danger lies with those unintended recipients who don't have a clue as to what drove the charged-up message to begin with. This leads them to negatively judge the originator of the email as someone they are not, placing that person in a very precarious position.

In conclusion, emails can do more harm than good.

As described above, they allow for what I call a virtual input-output disconnect. They open the door for the entire corporation to experience only the emotional output of a situation without having to first experience the input which drove those emotions. This is an incredibly dangerous trap, one that's nearly impossible to wiggle out of as the email which got the person here can *never be taken back.* It can however be prevented. You just have to be self-cognizant enough to realize when you're in an overly-charged emotional state and make yourself sit on the email for ten minutes prior to sending it. By doing so, you're giving your "emotional seesaw" time to balance back out in favor of rational thinking which will reverse your decision to send it ninety-nine out of one hundred times. And given the amount of email trouble I've had throughout my career, this is certainly a skill I wish I had possessed prior to my first day. Lucky for me none of my hiccups were enough to get me fired. Several of my coworkers were not so fortunate. Don't end up like them.

# IX: CONCLUSION

MANY CONCEPTS HAVE BEEN DISCUSSED throughout this book. If implemented correctly, they can all but guarantee your success within the confines of a major corporation. Below is a summarization of the most important points. Consider this a reference guide, broken down into three sections. The first will cover chapters two, three, and four. These chapters were designed to improve your mental awareness surrounding the human capital structure within corporations. Also covered was the dependency between types of work being done at different levels and how they support not only each other, but the corporation as a whole. This section provides your psychological foundation which must be solidified prior to advancing into the more complex strategies to follow. The second section covers chapters five, six, and seven. Reviewed here are specific psychological techniques that if implemented properly will fast-track your path to corporate stardom. And in the last section, the ten behaviors that you absolutely must avoid to ensure a smooth ride to the top.

### Psychological Foundation

*Chapter II: Your First Day – Get Your Head Straight*

- Your performance in college means nothing now. There are no carryovers.
- You are not powerless as a new employee. Corporations need you to survive.

- Make your expectations clear from day one if pursuing high-ranking positions. Your development will require specific experiences which the corporation must plan for.
- Only one person in the corporation cares about you. That person is *you*.
- You are no longer a human once inside a corporation. Instead, you are an asset and will be treated as such.
- Corporations cannot survive without capable leaders guiding them. Proving your ability to lead from day one will place you in extreme demand.

*Chapter III: The Corporate "Ski Lift"*

- People have expiration dates. Corporations do not. To survive indefinitely, corporations must continually cycle people throughout.
- Managing the flow of human capital within corporations is serious business. Succession plans are often used to help simplify the process.
- Similar to a ski lift, succession plans are built around the notion that employees come both on and off the "mountain" at all different levels, all at the same time.
- The speed at which these transitions occur must be closely managed and synchronized with current business demands. If not, too many or too few employees will be coming in or out of the business, causing productivity gaps.
- Corporations must also manage how far up the "mountain" employees are allowed to go. Higher levels come with greater complexity. Proper experience is required to successfully navigate the more difficult slopes.
- Salary should not be your focus early in your career.

Rather, it should be on attaining quality experiences. After several years of accumulation, these experiences will grant you access to higher levels with higher pay.

*Chapter IV: Respect—See the Invisible*

- When seeking a promotion, you must indirectly overpower your boss's authority to where they have no other option *but* to promote you.
- This is accomplished by ascending to the top of your organization's dominance hierarchy.
- Once achieved, you will be gifted the natural power of influence over your peers. You will then be identified by the corporation as one who can successfully guide others for the betterment of the organization. It's at this moment when a promotion, under perfect circumstances, *should* occur.
- Perfect circumstances rarely occur in corporations—the demand for your abilities must also be present. If not, you will become "oversupply" and remain at your current level both in organizational ranking and in pay. You will remain there until demand increases, even though your abilities may warrant a higher market value.
- Your company will never tell you that you aren't being paid true market value because of an oversupply situation. It's up to you to figure this out. Utilizing online business platforms like LinkedIn is the easiest way to do so. Keep your profile updated and interview with outside companies several times a year. Then compare their offers to your current compensation to see where you stand.
- Undersupply situations can also occur. Here, your demand will be abnormally high, forcing employers to pay a premium for your services as they have

nobody else to fall back on. For the ambitious types, aggressively seeking companies under these circumstances will ensure your compensation remains above average market rate.

- This can easily be done using recruiters and websites such as Glassdoor.com. Input your desired position and view compensation ranges from companies in your target area. Identify the maximum companies are paying and communicate your requirements to as many recruiters as possible and let them do the work for you.

- Be careful not to jump around too often. If possible, give each company three years' worth of employment. Doing so allows them to recoup their investment. It also prevents future employers from labeling you as someone who could be hiding chronic performance issues.

## Techniques for Success

*Chapter V: The Corporate Chameleon*

- To gain rank within the dominance hierarchy, you must become the most effective producer in your organization.

- This is accomplished by adapting to your coworker's psychological preferences.

- If adaptation is achieved, their "guard" will be dropped and access to their chapters in the corporate textbook will be granted.

- Each of these chapters represents specific knowledge about the business. You cannot complete your assignments without it.

- Psychological adaptation will grant you more than just business knowledge. Respect is also earned from your willingness to engage on your cowork-

ers' psychological terms, not yours.
- Once respect is earned, you are granted the power of influence over those who awarded you with it.
- Corporations desperately seek this skill when assessing candidates for higher paying leadership positions.
- Psychological adaptation doesn't end with your coworkers. You must also tailor your work products to fit within your bosses' psychological constraints. This will allow them to easily interpret your work and is how you become a "favorite".

*Chapter VI: The Battle Begins –*
*Let Your Army do the Dirty Work*

- There are only so many high-ranking positions to go around. As you gain rank in the dominance hierarchy, some will see it as a threat to their future career advancement. Dishonest attacks against your reputation may result.
- Similar to Amazon rankings, your reputation is the cumulative average score of your interactions with other coworkers. Management uses these scores to determine where employees rank within dominance hierarchy. Promotions are issued accordingly.
- Protecting your reputation is critical. *It's all you have.*
- Proper adaptation makes this protection easy. Once respect is earned, not only will you gain access to your coworkers' knowledge, but also their protection should your reputation be unfairly targeted.

*Chapter VIII: Clothing – Yes, An Entire Chapter*

- The final say for promotions is made by an executive way up the chain. Given the number of layers between them and the candidate, their interaction prior to this point is minimal at best.

- Because of this, corporations must find ways to expose candidates and their abilities to the executive. This allows for a higher degree of confidence when making the final decision.
- This exposure occurs through carefully crafted assignments specifically designed to provide opportunity for this interaction.
- In a perfect world, employees who rank at the top of their dominance hierarchy are selected for such assignments. But corporations don't always get things right.
- Every advantage must be used to ensure your selection. You cannot leave anything to chance. Your clothing choices are one such advantage.
- Clothing should not be considered an expense. Rather, an investment that will provide a future return.
- You don't have to spend a fortune—a quality wardrobe can be built on a budget. But you must start well in advance. Adequate time is required to capitalize on retailers during their weakest moments.
- Preparation is a critical skill that transfers throughout all of business. Showing up properly dressed on day one is an easy way to display such skills. The corporation may use this as a preliminary metric to determine how they issue those ever so critical starting assignments.
- Your clothing should deter attention, not attract it. Determine the psychological boundaries within your corporation and stay within your range.

## Behaviors to Avoid

*Chapter VIII: Corporate Landmines –
Watch Where You Step*

- Complacency kills. Treat every day like it's your first.
- It's good to be smart. But in corporations, your intelligence is limited to the bandwidth you are provided to exert it through. Be patient until you are given an open road.
- There will be countless initiatives pushed upon you as a corporate employee. Some you will agree with, some you won't. But one thing remains constant— they will *never* cease. You must play along regardless of personal preferences in order to survive.
- Meeting deadlines is important. But never let them interfere with the quality of your work. It will haunt you every time. Ten years from now, nobody will remember the deadlines you missed. But they will all remember the errors you made while doing so.
- Not all mistakes are bad. Those made when learning something new are your friend. Embrace them. But don't repeat them.
- We all have personal problems. Some worse than others. But never make the office aware of them. It can and will hinder your progression through the ranks. Fake it till you make it.
- As a corporate employee, you must immediately produce as soon as you're called upon to do so. Habitual procrastinators are quickly identified and filtered out of the company.
- Spread your wings wide. Never turn down an assignment, even if it's outside your specific responsibilities. Doing so will build your sponsor base and provide a safety net should your primary lifeline

unexpectedly disappear.
- You have two options when confronted with negative circumstances. If within your control, change them. If uncontrollable, find creative ways to deal with them. They can always be reversed in your favor if played correctly. But *never* try to control an uncontrollable.
- The greatest threat to your corporate longevity is your email account. Only send *when required* and never while in an emotionally charged state of mind. They can and will get you fired.

———◆———

That's all I have. I hope you enjoyed the read. Writing this has played a major part of my life for the last seven years, though I quit on it several times during that period. But each time I did, life would push me back to the keyboard. Messages from above, perhaps. Whatever they were, they provided me the strength to persevere, allowing me to finish what I hope to be the most helpful resource ever made for those entering a major corporation for the first time. With that, thank you for your time, thank you for your support, and most of all, thank you for reading.

*-David*

DEAR READER: FOR THOSE WHO may be wondering what the next step is, please visit Corporations101.com where I will continue writing about life inside major corporations. I have plenty of additional fodder to cover. Also, if you enjoyed my writing and feel compelled to help me on my journey, please share my blog using the buttons provided on the page.

Made in the USA
Monee, IL
28 October 2020